CITIZENSHIP EDUCATION AND THE PERSONALIZATION OF DEMOCRACY

The core message of this book is that democracy is, more than ever before, in need of the personal contributions of engaged citizens. Democracy is viable only if it is rooted in the hearts and minds of citizens who feel responsible not only for their own well-being, but also for the quality of social relationships in a society with marked differences in race, religion, culture, and gender.

Three basic features define personalized democracy: A critical attitude not only towards others but also towards oneself; learning not only from others but also from oneself; and participation in society with attention to the contradictive nature of one's own mind. The authors emphasize that the development of personalized democracy and global citizenship requires participation at different levels of identity: I as individual; we as members of social groups; we as part of humanity; and we as part of the Earth. Written for future teachers at secondary level, the book contains dialogical self theory, research, and a wide range of exercises.

Hubert J.M. Hermans is professor emeritus of psychology at Radboud University of Nijmegen, The Netherlands. He is honorary president of the International Society for Dialogical Science and creator of Dialogical Self Theory. For his scientific merits he was decorated as Knight in the Order of the Netherlands Lion. He is first author of more than 200 books and articles in scientific journals.

Rob Bartels is a lecturer and teacher trainer in Philosophy and Educational Sciences. He wrote his PhD dissertation on the subject of The Contribution of Philosophy with Children to Democratic Education.

CITIZENSHIP EDUCATION AND THE PERSONALIZATION OF DEMOCRACY

Hubert J.M. Hermans and Rob Bartels

NEW YORK AND LONDON

First published 2021
by Routledge
52 Vanderbilt Avenue, New York, NY 10017

and by Routledge
2 Park Square, Milton Park, Abingdon, Oxon OX14 4RN

Routledge is an imprint of the Taylor & Francis Group, an informa business

© 2021 Taylor & Francis

The right of Hubert J.M. Hermans and Rob Bartels to be identified as authors of this work has been asserted by them in accordance with sections 77 and 78 of the Copyright, Designs and Patents Act 1988.

All rights reserved. No part of this book may be reprinted or reproduced or utilised in any form or by any electronic, mechanical, or other means, now known or hereafter invented, including photocopying and recording, or in any information storage or retrieval system, without permission in writing from the publishers.

Trademark notice: Product or corporate names may be trademarks or registered trademarks, and are used only for identification and explanation without intent to infringe.

Library of Congress Cataloging-in-Publication Data
Names: Hermans, H. J. M., author. | Bartels, Rob, 1953- author.
Title: Citizenship education and the personalization of democracy /
    Hubert J.M. Hermans, Rob Bartels.
Description: New York, NY : Routledge, 2021. | Includes bibliographical
    references and index.
Identifiers: LCCN 2020029652 (print) | LCCN 2020029653 (ebook) |
    ISBN 9780367467906 (hardback) | ISBN 9780367467890 (paperback) |
    ISBN 9781003031116 (ebook)
Subjects: LCSH: Citizenship–Study and teaching. | Democracy–Study and
    teaching. | Political participation.
Classification: LCC LC1091 .H37 2021 (print) | LCC LC1091 (ebook) |
    DDC 370.11/5–dc23
LC record available at https://lccn.loc.gov/2020029652
LC ebook record available at https://lccn.loc.gov/2020029653

ISBN: 978-0-367-46790-6 (hbk)
ISBN: 978-0-367-46789-0 (pbk)
ISBN: 978-1-003-03111-6 (ebk)

Typeset in Bembo
by Taylor & Francis Books

CONTENTS

List of Figures	*vii*
List of Tables	*ix*
List of Boxes	*x*
About the Authors	*xi*
Acknowledgements	*xiii*
Introduction	*xiv*

PART 1
Opposition   1

1	*I*-Positions: Who Are You and Where Are You?	3
2	Are You Tolerant of Alternative Viewpoints?	11
3	Suspension of Judgment: Why is it So Difficult?	19
4	Flexible Change of Perspective: Be flexible like a dancer	25
5	Meta-positions: Look at Yourself as if from a Helicopter in the Sky	32
6	Tolerance of Uncertainty: Helpful or Unhelpful?	41
7	Emotion and Reason: Can They Hold Hands?	52
	Epilogue to Part 1	62

vi Contents

PART 2
Cooperation   **67**

8 Learning from Yourself   69

9 The Power of Listening   79

10 When Values Matter   86

11 Depolarizing Opposition   94

12 From Debate to Dialogue   105

13 Empathy: A Frequently Used Word, but Difficult to Express   115

   Epilogue to Part 2   125

PART 3
Participation   **129**

14 Four Levels of Identity: Are You Just an Individual, or More
   than That?   131

15 From Group Identity to Human Identity: What Does it Mean
   when You Call Yourself "Human"?   139

16 Are We Masters of the Earth or Part of It?   147

17 How Can We Promote Inner Democracy?   155

18 What Obstructs our Inner Democracy?   166

   Epilogue to Part 3   177

References   *181*
Appendix   *187*
Index   *189*

FIGURES

0.1	Plea for democracy	xix
1.1	What is democracy?	5
1.2	Others as external *I*-positions in ourselves	7
1.3	Venn diagram	9
2.1	Valley of open-mindedness	13
3.1	Photo from Unsplash	24
4.1	Changing your *I*-position needs a flexible mind	28
5.1	Take some time off to see the big picture and your direction in life	34
5.2	The "power" of consumer-citizens	36
6.1	Shall we survive?	45
6.2	Uncertainty requires us to explore different roads	49
7.1	Location of the prefrontal cortex and amygdala	55
7.2	Disliked groups and their percentages	57
7.3	*This is what we die for*	60
8.1	Moments of self-consultation	72
8.2	Task-related self-criticism improves your performance	74
9.1	Active listening requires full attention	81
10.1	Do we use existing knowledge or not?	87
10.2	Cultural diversity and togetherness	90
10.3	If you could decide, what would you say?	93
11.1	How to solve a conflict?	96
11.2	How to eliminate your enemies?	100
12.1	Debate	106

viii List of Figures

12.2	Dialogue (replaced by electronic communication in corona-time)	107
12.3	Talking stick	110
13.1	How can you cultivate compassion in your life?	117
13.2	Empathy requires eye contact and listening in an open way	121
14.1	Levels of inclusiveness	133
14.2	Paintings from Vassily Kandinsky and Paul Klee	134
14.3	Distress and helplessness after a school shooting	136
15.1	One group, yet very different individuals	142
16.1	Caring for the Earth	152
16.2	How precious is biodiversity?	154
17.1	Open questions are indispensable for a constructive dialogue	157
17.2	In the course of evolution, we *Homo sapiens* have become a question to ourselves—we need a flexible mind to deal with our impulses	161
18.1	Body-building arm with an imagined kiss	169
18.2	The seductive power of grandiose utopias	171
18.3	Scale of justice	176

TABLES

0.1	Sections within each chapter and their content	xxiii
12.1	Differences between debate and dialogue	112
16.1	Different levels of inclusiveness	151

BOXES

Hong Kong, China, and the lack of open-mindedness	14
Consumer-Citizen: A Powerful Coalition	35
The Paradox of Solomon	38
Responses to uncertainty are highly different	43
Aladdin and the wonderful lamp	88
Theory of mind	116
School shootings as the ultimate end of non-participation	135
The Pianist	140
Music as spreading a new morality	148

ABOUT THE AUTHORS

Hubert J.M. Hermans is emeritus professor of psychology at the Radboud University of Nijmegen, The Netherlands. His dissertation "Motivation and achievement" (1967) resulted in the construction of several psychological tests for measuring achievement motivation and fear of failure. As a reaction to the static and impersonal nature of psychological tests, he developed a Self-Confrontation Method, published in the book *Self-Narratives* by Guilford Press (1995). In the 1990s he developed the internationally known Dialogical Self Theory, inspired by the American pragmatism of William James and the dialogical school of the Russian literary scholar Mikhail Bakhtin. In 2002 he was decorated as Knight in the Order of the Netherlands Lion for exceptional scientific achievements in the service of society. His Dutch book *Dialoog en misverstand* [*Dialogue and misunderstanding*] (2006) was used by Herman Wijffels during the preparation of the Dutch government (Balkenende 4, 2007). He is Honorary Associate of the Taos Institute (2012) and was elected as international member of the Royal Flemish Academy of Belgium for Sciences and the Arts (2018). He is president of the International Society for Dialogical Science.

Rob Bartels is an experienced college professor and education specialist. After many years as a primary school teacher in The Netherlands, he specialized in Philosophy with Children and has a Master's degree in educational pedagogy. His PhD in educational sciences involved a thesis on the contribution of Philosophy with Children to the development of democratic skills and attitudes. He is a college teacher (since 2001) and a researcher on democratic education (since 2004). As a college teacher he specializes in designing educational curricula and learning programs, and is jointly responsible for the construction of curricula for primary school teachers. He teaches educational psychology and the design of xii About the Authors

learning trajectories. He has published several books on Philosophy with Children, and articles on democratic education. He is a partner in the Dutch Centre for Philosophy with Children and an executive board member of the Sophia Network, the European Foundation for the Advancement of Doing Philosophy with Children.

ACKNOWLEDGEMENTS

First, we wish to thank our colleague Anti Bax, who has translated this book from Dutch to English. She has also edited the whole text in detail, and enriched it with her numerous creative ideas and suggestions for improvement of the content.

We also thank Jessica Cooke, Matthew Friberg, and Ilaria Tassistro of Routledge for their excellent guidance during the process of preparing and publishing this book.

INTRODUCTION

Citizenship education and the personalization of democracy

The basic motive for writing this book is that contemporary society needs young adults who learn to personalize democracy, that is, to make citizenship an integral part of their everyday lives. Why? Given the recent spread of nationalism in many countries around the world, and the increasing trend toward authoritarianism, teachers and educators are becoming more and more aware of the necessity of citizenship education with special attention to critical thinking, personal and social responsibility, and ecological awareness. A recent report of the International Association for the Evaluation of Educational Achievement (Schulz et al., 2018) summarizes research in secondary schools in 24 countries under the title *Becoming citizens in a changing world*. The study found that the three goals teachers deemed most important for their students' development were: promoting students' critical and independent thinking (61%); promoting students' knowledge of citizens' rights and responsibilities (57%); and promoting respect for and safeguard of the environment (51%) (p. xvi).

The present publication endorses these aims, and adds a significant *psychological* dimension. It promotes not only critical thinking in general, but also self-critical thinking, in that it invites students to examine their own beliefs, values, and identities.[1] As authors, we aim to emphasize not only the responsibilities of citizens in general, but also their own personal and social responsibilities as world citizens. Moreover, we want to enhance respect for the environment and stimulate the development of an "ecological identity" that makes students aware that they themselves are part of the Earth. The book achieves these aims by providing critical information about basic democratic principles, but also—even primarily—by personalizing democracy, exploring students' experiences in their own lives through thought-provoking questions, guiding concepts, self-quizzes, exciting games, and interactive exercises. The book is written in language that is accessible to undergraduate and graduate educational levels in higher education, and at the same time refers to situations in students' own personal lives.

Why is such a book urgent? In general, democracy has long been considered as one of the most precious achievements of contemporary society. In marked contrast to this view is the recent finding that presently there is, in many countries, dissatisfaction regarding the actual functioning of democracy. In a 2018 international survey across 27 nations by the Pew Research Center (Kent, 2019), it appeared that, overall, people were more dissatisfied than satisfied with the way democracy is working in their countries. Although the satisfaction was high in some countries (e.g., Sweden, Indonesia, the Philippines), it was very low in others (e.g., Mexico, Greece, Brazil). Even in the USA, traditionally seen as the democratic pinnacle of our civilization, more respondents were dissatisfied than satisfied. The finding that the average dissatisfaction across the nations under investigation was higher than the rate of satisfaction may serve as a wake-up call to all those who are devoted to basic democratic principles.

Despite these findings, citizens generally have a strong preference for such democratic principles as freedom of speech, freedom of elections, and the right to demonstrate. Many people believe that the world is a better place with protection of civil rights by democratic institutions such as parliamentary systems, judiciary systems, and the rule of law. But is it enough to merely *endorse* these privileges that our recent history has offered us?

What difference can this book make?

We argue in this book that we need to do much more than just *agree* with democracy. A democratic society needs citizens who want more than just expressing their preference for free elections, freedom of speech, and constitutional rights. These conditions are too non-committal to develop a society in which people interact with each other in a genuinely democratic way. Democracy is only vital if it is rooted in the personal, experiential world of the people who live in such societies. This is exactly the core message of this book. It is not intended to enhance *knowledge* about democracy, but to explore and develop your personal democratic *attitude*. This attitude involves not only the way you interact with important people in your immediate environment, but also with how you think and feel about other groups in society. It also touches on the way you interact with yourself, and how you react to your own emotions when confronted with serious political debates and discussions. In this book, you will start to explore how you might develop tolerance and understanding for individuals and groups who differ from you. But you will also learn to explore the thoughts and emotions aroused within you by the "otherness" of someone else, and what responses this might trigger in you.

This book gives you instruments to explore your democratic attitude in relation to other people and yourself—and it also wants to help you stimulate and further develop this attitude. It invites you in the first place to explore what democracy means in your own personal life. Then, through background information, you will be given questions, exercizes, and other means to give your democratic attitude an extra stimulant. This is, in a nutshell, what developing "inner democracy" means: to further your personal democratic attitude in relation to yourself and other people. After all, within your inner self you can also act in a more or less democratic manner. This manifests itself in the acknowledgement and tolerance of inner conflicts and inner contrary viewpoints in your contact with other people who hold different opinions, viewpoints, and motivations. Inner democracy, then, means that we acquire knowledge about conflicting points of view and learn how to respond to them in a way that does justice to ourselves and other people.

Along this route, this book aims to contribute to the development of *personal citizenship.* This form of citizenship is more than just knowledge about your rights and duties in society. It addresses the way you shape democracy in your interactions with yourself, and with individuals and groups who are different from you. In this context, we give ample attention to the fundamental importance of dialogue: In what respect can you, and do you want to, entertain a dialogical relationship with other people and with your own self? This implies that you can learn to listen in an attentive way to other people, and that you acknowledge the impulses and emotions invoked in you and learn how you can respond to these emotions. A productive inner dialogue promotes a mutually productive relationship between reason and emotion. Democracy doesn't just occur in a voting place, but also, and especially, at home, at school, on the street, and at moments when you start an inner dialogue and start your own self-exploration.

In that self-exploration you will begin to investigate the different ways you can deal with situations in your own society—as a student in relation to your teachers, as a student in relation to your fellow students, as a sports fanatic in relation to other sports lovers, as a contact on Facebook, and in your relationships with different cultural groups that are part of our global society. We call the various ways you assume a position in relation to other persons "*I*-positions," and you will learn in this book that all those *I*-positions are more or less democratically organized. They all want to have a justified place in your life. One of the most striking new ideas of this book is that the *inner society of I-positions* forms a micro-society that is a part of society at large, and that this micro-society can also be democratically organized. The way you organize your life has direct implications for the way you deal with other individuals, and with the *I*-positions within yourself. When we talk about *I*-positions, we also have "we-positions" in mind, as "I" and "we" are often intimately related. In this book we explore the connection between your personal inner life and the relations you maintain with other people in society, as reflected in the book's title: *Citizenship Education and the Personalization of Democracy*.

The basic message behind this title is to stimulate an awareness that you are an important agent in our society. Your engagement is needed. It is important to know who you are, how you are shaped by the world as a member of a functioning democracy, and how you define your own role as a participating member in this world.

The structure of the book

From our assumption that democracy starts in yourself, we propose that the basic principles—*opposition, cooperation,* and *participation*—are timely and relevant in situations where international media refer to growing nationalist and populist movements and divisive identity struggles. Although these trends may express an explicit or implicit desire for the protection of national and group identities in a globalizing world, they typically seek to divide communities and countries along the lines of citizenship, race, language, and nationality. This indicates the urgency of global conversations about how we understand our personal role in democracy and global citizenship.

Opposition (Part 1)

A democratic society cannot exist without opposition or conflict. Democracy can be vital and viable only when space is given to individuals or groups who hold points of view regarding political and societal concerns that differ from the majority. A fully grown democracy is characterized by respect for minorities and by being open to their viewpoints, possibilities, and desires. Discussion, competition, and conflicting arguments all offer possibilities in bringing together a diversity of opinions and ways of exploring them. Democracy allows alternative voices to be expressed and to be taken seriously, even when they conflict with each other.

A fundamental argument of this book is that we don't apply opposition just to democracy at large, but also, in the form of inner opposition, we apply it to the relations we have within ourselves. Inner democracy implies that participants in a society are capable of opposition not just to other individuals, but also within themselves. In this book, we invite you to explore how you can allow yourself to react in a critical way to other individuals, and also to different voices within yourself. When you allow opposition within yourself in a productive way, and when you are capable of correcting or nuancing some of your original opinions, then space opens up to escape from your own bubble and explore alternative opinions and viewpoints on their own merits, both toward other individuals as well as toward yourself. This book challenges you to leave your comfort zone and assume, temporarily, the point of view of someone else who has a different

xviii Introduction

opinion, and from there to change or broaden your original opinions without relinquishing your original point of view altogether.

Cooperation (Part 2)

In a democratic society, it is not possible to move on when faced with only conflict and opposition. There should be a moment when you come to cooperation. In that cooperation, space needs to be given to discuss central themes of society that ask for solutions or answers (e.g., climate change, the power of digital giants' communication platforms, immigration). Along this route, coalitions can arise among parties or groups that contribute their own answers to these questions and explore possible solutions. When a constructive coalition arises, the participants can *learn* something from each other that was not present beforehand. This learning from each other applies not only in the political realm, but everywhere where people live or work together: at work, in school, in the family, or a sports club. Working and living together requires a continuous learning process in which you let someone else express certain views from which you can learn something you didn't know beforehand, or even something that is completely new for you.

A basic characteristic of inner democracy is that we learn not only from each other, but also (and closely related to it) from ourselves. When it comes to learning, we observe that we do not pick up much new information from friends who just pat us on the head, compared with opponents who make critical comments about our behavior and beliefs. Critique or revision can also come from a friend or fellow student who has the courage to tell us things we do not very much like to hear. Such remarks can haunt us, we remember them, and we will keep walking around for a while with those comments. Time to learn! Our most stubborn opponents are the emotions that arise when we are challenged by criticism or painful comments. That is a possible turning point. Do we give priority to the negative emotion and ignore the opposing voice, or do we move forward through that emotion and turn it to our advantage? That is why we pay a lot of attention in this book to the concept of inner dialogue between emotion and reason as a prerequisite for a learning process and as a source of self-correction and self-innovation.

Participation (Part 3)

When we are making room for opposition, and consequently learning from each other in cooperative endeavors, then active participation of citizens in a globalizing society is essential. Participation emerges by exercising rights (e.g., freedom of speech, freedom of religion, giving each other equal rights) and obligations in relation to society (e.g., complying with the law, offering help in emergencies,

FIGURE 0.1 Plea for democracy
Source: Unsplash

paying taxes). If citizens are not willing to comply with their obligations and accept responsibilities, if they do not abide by the law, and if they are not willing to make their contribution to a "good society," then we can no longer speak of a democracy.

xx Introduction

Participation is a guiding principle in society at large, and also within our inner selves. Divergent situations invoke in us different *I*-positions. These function not just as roles we play in social interactions (as a parent, an employee, a student). They can also be personal, as in a situation where we react in a deviant way when we feel we are treated unjustly. They are also personal if we are cooperative when someone asks for our help, or when we share a secret with a friend. All these *I*-positions demand attention because each one of them, in a particular situation, plays a role in our inner society of mind.

Participation in a localized and globalized world has important consequences for the definition of citizenship. Traditionally, citizenship is defined as "the status of a person recognized under the custom or law as being a legal citizen of a sovereign state or belonging to a nation."[2] For participation as an engaged citizen in a globalizing world, a broader definition is required. We propose a definition of *multilevel citizenship* that, closely associated with identity formation, functions at different levels of inclusion: (a) I as an individual; (b) I as a group member; (c) I as part of humanity; and (d) I as part of the Earth. The advantage of this conception is that it broadens citizenship beyond the individual level (I as an individual) and beyond the group level (e.g., I as belonging to this nation, or my ethnic identity). It also gives space to I as a representative of humanity, who is able and willing to act as a global citizen in a highly interconnected world. And, crucial in a period of climate change, it has the potential of making people aware that they are part of the Earth. We will argue in Part 3 of this book that each of these levels coexists with specific responsibilities: personal responsibility (I as an individual person), social responsibility (I as a citizen of this country), collective responsibility (I as a global citizen), and ecological responsibility (I as part of the Earth). A democratic citizen develops the capacity to *move flexibly from one level of inclusion to another*, contingent on the demands of the situation at hand and, correspondingly, is able to respond with different kinds of responsibility as the result of an inner dialogue. The innovative implication of this view is that citizenship is not something you "have" ("possess") as a member of a country, state, or city viewed as an "external" community. The central idea is that you are also, and even primarily, a citizen of your own society of mind, which participates, at the same time, in society at large.

In this micro-society we find *I*-positions that have an important influence on society at large. An example we describe in this book is the relation between 'I as a consumer' (individual level) and 'I as a global citizen' (collective level). These positions are sometimes in conflict with each other in situations where we need to make a choice. A certain choice demands an inner dialogue that determines the ultimate result of the choice we make in a specific situation (e.g., I know that our food choices have a direct impact on the future of the rainforests, but I like to eat meat: what do I do?).

The recent outbreak of the coronavirus pandemic that has shocked the world order, and will alter it in the long term, adds to the necessity for a multi-level citizenship. As Alemanno (2020) writes, the COVID-19 infection is not the first, nor will it be the last, of a series of real or potential catastrophes—be they pandemics, natural disasters, or terrorist attacks—that have taken us by surprise. No other emergency has led to such disruptive lockdown measures worldwide, paralysing the world economy and unveiling the gap between global economic interdependence and nation-state governance. No other risk management response has raised so many novel legal, ethical, moral, and political issues. No other pandemic has been covered continually by a 24-hour news cycle, amplified by social media users, often reporting conflicting information simultaneously. No other crisis has suddenly reshaped our individual and collective ideas of uncertainty and risk. Ultimately, no other event has carried this potential to disrupt our democratic, economic, legal, social, and cultural systems. These developments pose an unprecedented challenge to our multi-level citizenship. This challenge dramatically affects not only our individual lives, but also relationships between social groups, as economically disadvantaged groups are afflicted more seriously than more advantaged ones. The awareness that we are highly interdependent on a global scale requires us to give a response to the pandemic that transcends the boundaries of any social, political, or national group. This new situation compels us to think not only as individuals or group members, but also as members of humankind as the broadest level of our solidarity. The pandemic has even an impact on an ecological level as it alters our relationship with animals, nature, and the Earth itself. So we emphasize in Part 3 of this book that the development of inner democracy requires our participation at different identity levels: I as individual, we as members of social groups, we as part of humanity, and we as part of the Earth.

The foregoing shows that there is a close relation between external democracy in society at large, and internal democracy in the micro-society of *I*-positions and we-positions within ourselves. Basic characteristics, such as opposition, cooperation, and participation, can be applied in both domains, whereby communication channels arise that facilitate flexible movement back and forth from one domain to the other. The result is that self and society are no longer considered as separate components (my own little world versus big society), but as parts of a self-and-society interconnection. The self is a micro-society that not only "moves along with" changes in the macro-society, but also influences that society as being part of it, in a more or less productive way.

Pedagogical foundation

From a pedagogical point of view, the book is inspired by John Dewey's (1938) three democratic principles, as elaborated in their practical implications by MacMath (2008): (a) all human beings are morally equal; (b) we can solve any problem if we work collaboratively; and (c) we are all capable of forming intelligent and well-informed opinions.

xxii Introduction

The principle of *moral equality* implies that student-relevant histories have an equal place within the curriculum. This means that students should be able to see their multicultural histories reflected in school curricula. Teachers are invited to actively seek out the multicultural experiences of their students and give that information a place in the curriculum. Empowerment of students is derived from knowledge and social relations that each respect their own histories, languages, and cultural traditions. In this sense, democracy is linked to transformative dialogue and actions that have the potential to alter the oppressive conditions in which marginalized groups in our society are living. This means a shift from traditional definitions of society in terms of a strictly political agenda of national government, to considering democracy as a transformative tool for citizens to re-imagine their society. The principle of moral equality functions as the pedagogical basis of Part 1 of this book, which deals with *opposition* and space for discussion between individuals and groups who are considered as equal human beings from a moral point of view.

In order to realize the *principle of collaboration*, students are invited to listen to others, to share their opinions and thoughts, and to provide peer assessment and feedback. A democratic pedagogy implies that students are engaged in a collaborative dialogue in which they are encouraged to discuss controversial issues and become involved in teamwork. These practices not only need to permeate the classroom, they also exist between the classroom and the community at large. The community can be brought into the classroom by inviting local speakers or local politicians, and the students can orient themselves to the community. This "outward-looking" community approach is defined broadly, including not only interactions with other individuals and groups, but also local and global connections. Local community members can be brought into the classroom for presentations and projects; global connections can be made by communicating with students in other countries through the internet and multimedia. The principle of collaboration is a central issue in Part 2 that focuses on *cooperation*.

The *principle of developing intelligent and well-informed opinions* is essential in Dewey's assertion that reflection, as a method of intelligence, is central to a democracy where citizens participate in the reconstruction of values so that they find a basis in themselves to decide what to believe and what not to believe. To make informed judgments, explicit instructions in critical thinking are needed, as well as opportunities to practice decision-making. Explicit instructions in critical thinking require the capacity to take in multiple perspectives while simultaneously making connections between these perspectives. Explicit instructions are required to help students define and develop various fundamental mindsets. These mindsets include "awareness of one's own thinking processes, inquisitiveness, fair-mindedness, tolerance, sensitivity, open-mindedness, persistence, and the ability to set goals and make plans" (Kassem, 2000, p. 31). The principle of forming intelligent and well-informed opinions is the pedagogical basis of Part 3 on *participation*.

Methodology

Each of the three parts of this book (opposition, cooperation, and participation) comprises five to seven chapters in which the idea of inner democracy is further explored. In each chapter we apply the principle of "circular learning," not very different from Kolb's (1984) theory of experiential learning. We ask you at the beginning of a chapter what you know about a certain topic and what your experiences are, for instance, about empathy, polarization, or narcissism. Then we give background information about these specific topics and describe what is known about that subject in the scientific literature. As a response to this information, we give you the opportunity to ask critical questions about the content of that specific chapter. The knowledge you have acquired in that chapter, as well as your reflections, can be discussed with your fellow students.

At the end of each chapter we present some *exercises* in which you can apply what you have learned. You can do these exercises together with your fellow students under the guidance of the teacher, so you can discuss the results with each other. Sometimes we will offer exercises that you can do individually. The purpose of the exercises is to apply the theoretical insights you have learned to everyday situations, and we offer you specific guidelines about the various ways you can do this. And finally, there is an opportunity for *reflection*, the intention of which is to close the circle and make the connection between what you have learned and your prior knowledge.

We present the substance of the book in 18 short chapters. In those chapters we describe certain basic concepts (e.g., "*I*-position," "boundaries of the self," "consumption") in various different contexts. Inspired by the principle of *distributed learning* (Kang, 2016; Kreijns et al., 2004), we will return to these concepts repeatedly in the successive chapters so you can apply them in various different situations. This helps you to apply the concepts in different situations in a flexible manner, but also to store them in long-term memory.

To strengthen the memory storage of what has been learned so far, at the end of each Part we give a *self-quiz* consisting of 10 multiple-choice questions to check if you have correctly digested the background information. To pass the

TABLE 0.1 Sections within each chapter and their content

Section	Description
From your own experience	What have you already experienced?
Background information	What is known about this topic in the literature?
Critical questions	Inviting you to look critically at the preceding text
Exercises	Practices to bridge knowing and doing
Reflecting	Returning to your own experience: What has changed?

xxiv Introduction

quiz, you need to give at least 7 correct answers to the 10 questions. In case you do not pass the test, you are invited to re-examine the chapters of that Part and answer the quiz questions again. The correct answers are included in the appendix at the end of the book. This method ensures that you get specific feedback about the level of your knowledge regarding a certain topic, and that you have mastered the content of the chapters.

Readership

The intended readers of this book are educators at BA and MA college and university level and their students as prospective teachers at elementary and secondary school levels. The primary focus will be future teachers at secondary level, with those who teach at elementary level as the secondary focus. We have created a website that includes specific guidelines, practices, and exercises that are helpful to apply the subjects and topics of the book at both elementary and secondary levels.

The book will be particularly useful for the following target groups:

- Teachers and students of courses on Civic and Citizenship Education (CCE). This subject is taught in various education programs in the emerging area of civic studies and in teacher-education programs in Schools of Education. While civics relates to civic knowledge, citizenship is defined more broadly and addresses attitudes, values, dispositions, and skills. Citizenship is the primary focus of our book. The tenor of our book can be found in Wikipedia's article on "Civic education in the United States" (read May 11, 2019) which explains that 21st-century education has shifted to reflect young people's "personally expressive politics" and "peer-to-peer relationships" that promote citizenship engagement. This is exactly what we promote in our book.
- Students. Teacher training in pedagogy as a discipline and practice implies teaching children and young students to learn to develop themselves not only as individuals but also as citizens of the larger community. Young students will learn about themselves (with a focus on personal responsibility), what it means to engage with the social world around them (social responsibility), how to become constructive and contributing members of society at large (collective responsibility), and how to be ecologically aware citizens (ecological responsibility).
- Teachers/professors and their students in Schools of Education. We focus on professional teacher-education programs leading to Master of Arts (MA), Master of Education (MEd), or Master of Arts in Teaching (MAT) degrees at both undergraduate and graduate levels; and introductory government and political science classes and courses that are taught in the first year of Political Science curricula. The book will also be useful as a reference for instructors teaching introductory courses on Government/Civics.

- Teachers of psychology. As the book includes many psychological topics, it can also be used by teachers of psychology who are interested in the interface of psychology and political science. In particular, we think of courses in political psychology.
- English Education. Finally, we see this book as a supplementary text in English Education classrooms where teaching about equity, diversity, and issues of social justice is promoted. The book is also useful for helping students gain insight into their identity formation via the specific methods described above.

The book is written "in the language of the student" and is usable at the undergraduate level at freshman, sophomore, junior, and senior levels. At the graduate level, the book can be used for students who want to pursue a Master's or PhD degree in education. Depending on the nature of the specific curriculum, it can be used in courses for students pursuing a degree with a major or double major, or who do advanced course work at graduate level.

In short

The goal of the method chosen for this book is to build a bridge between democracy at large and democracy in ourselves. We consider this micro-democracy as a necessary ingredient for democracy at large, from the point of view that a vital democracy needs to have its roots in the fertile soil of our personal thoughts, emotions, and experiences. With the help of the three concepts—opposition, cooperation, and participation—we are building a bridge between self and society, as a way to relate macro-democracy and inner democracy. Because democracy in general is considered as an essential asset in our society, it makes sense to establish a connection between the way we interact with each other in society and the way we relate to ourselves, our personal experiences, thoughts, and emotions.[3] This can all be summarized with the slogan that democracy should not be endorsed, but lived.

Notes

1. See also Johnson & Morris (2010) who include values and identities in their concept of critical citizenship.
2. See "citizenship" as defined by Caves (2004), p. 97.
3. The scientific basis of the concept of inner democracy is explored in two works by Hubert J.M. Hermans: *Society in the self* (Hermans, 2018) and *Inner democracy* (Hermans, 2020). For personalizing politics see also Caprara & Vecchione's (2017) book *Personalizing politics and realizing democracy*.

PART 1

Opposition

1

I-POSITIONS: WHO ARE YOU AND WHERE ARE YOU?

In this first chapter we are going to investigate the meaning of "*I*-positions." Our "I" manifests itself in different situations in different ways—in other words, in different positions. Those different positions occur because our "I" does not always stand in the same relation to other people, who themselves also occupy their own *I*-positions. Other individuals can awaken different *I*-positions in us. How does this work? What is the meaning of the notion of an *I*-position?

From Your Own Experience

We are frequently aware of how other people think about us and perceive us. When you have to give a presentation in class, or when you have a job interview, you are not just thinking about what you should say, but also about how you would like others to perceive you, and what they think about you. Am I easy-going enough? Will they think of me as someone who is very motivated? Hopefully they will not notice that I am shy or timid. In fact, we frequently encounter situations in which we want other people to think differently about us compared to the image we have of ourselves.

Try to describe a situation—not that long ago—when you wanted to display a different image of yourself to other individuals.

Try to describe that situation in some catchy phrases:

- What kind of situation was it?
- Who was involved?
- Which characteristics of yourself did you want to show to others?

4 Part 1 Opposition

- Which specific characteristics did you want to emphasize in that situation?
- Was it difficult for you to do so?
- Do you think you were as successful as you wanted in how you came across to other individuals?
- Looking back on this situation, can you tell if you were yourself in that moment? Or in fact not? And why do you think this was the case?

Background Information

What is an I-position?

Suppose you are in contact with someone who asks for your help. If you agree to help that person, then you present yourself as a "helping person" or "facilitator." In another situation, you experience a conflict with another person and you let her know that you fundamentally disagree with her. And again in another situation, you are fascinated by the story that this other person tells, and you show your interest via your body language and your verbal comments. These are three examples of situations in which you "position" yourself in a certain way with regard to another person. To position yourself means that you assume a certain stance toward another individual. Depending on the specific situation, those positions can vary enormously in scope. In the above-mentioned examples you are, in succession, in different *I*-positions: "I as helper," "I as disagreeing," and "I as interested listener." These are examples of the various ways in which you relate to your social environment.

And, vice versa, other people can also position themselves in different ways towards you. The person to whom you position yourself as a helper might indicate that he very much likes the help you are offering. He is then in the position of "I as thankful." But it can also happen that this person feels uncomfortable with your offer of help. Giving help is often easier than receiving help. People often feel there is an expectation of a reward when help is offered to them. In that case, the person is grateful for your offer to help but cannot accept it. In the other example, in which you take a "disagreeing" stance, the other person can react as a "yes-man," but it can also be the case that he positions himself as a die-hard opponent. What develops depends on which position you assume and the position that the other person chooses in response to it. The response of the other person we call a "counter-position." Broadly defined, a counter-position is a response that is, more or less, different from one's own position. A counter-position can, in certain circumstances, be described as constructive and cooperative, but in other circumstances it can take the form of a conflict or sharp disagreement and can even lead to escalation. To assume certain *I*-positions is part and parcel of a process of positioning and counter-positioning.

Positioning in Relation to Yourself

An essential ingredient in the theory that this book proposes is that we are not only positioning ourselves relative to other individuals, but also within ourselves. Consider the example of the person who politely refuses your offer to help him. Something is going on in the inner self of this person. For instance, he appreciates your offer to help and would really like to accept it, but he has a problem with developing a dependency-relation. The position "I as receiving help" gets a counter-reaction to the position "I as an independent individual." If the latter position manifests itself as a stronger one, he will politely refuse your offer of help. The same process of positioning and counter-positioning can also play a role in your inner self.

Moreover, *I*-positions are not independent of each other. Just as a society consists of multiple individuals, with some more influential than others, the self is occupied by numerous *I*-positions in which some positions can dominate others. We can illustrate this with the following example. You are listening to someone who is giving a very elaborate monologue, and that other person doesn't care much if you want to hear all that she is saying. If you follow your impulse, you would say "this doesn't interest me at all." This position gets overshadowed by "I as a polite listener." This person is important to you, and you want to give her the opportunity to tell her story. And thus you let her continue on with her monologue. A more extreme example is where a person is addicted to games, drugs, certain kinds of food, or buying stuff, or is no longer able to resist the

FIGURE 1.1 What is democracy?
Source: Wikimedia Commons

seductive power of social media. This can result in an inner conflict. On one hand you are saying to yourself: I want to be free and determine for myself what I want or choose. On the other hand, you are no longer able to control yourself and you become engulfed in an addiction. In that case, the position of "I as master of myself" becomes dominated by "I as addicted" (assuming that you have the courage to acknowledge this to yourself). The counter-position, "master over myself," is no longer capable of keeping itself under control or correcting the undesirable position of "I as addicted."

Being Positioned by the Other

We not only position ourselves with regard to other individuals, we also get positioned by other individuals. Someone might give me a compliment for something that I have accomplished, and then I feel appreciated ("I as good"). However, if somebody accuses me of something, then that person positions himself as an accuser. And this can then lead to a counter-position from my side: I become defensive or even attack the other person. What is happening here is a process in which you get positioned by someone else whereupon you respond with a counter-position. This is an exchange between two persons. But assume that a possible counter-attack from my side gets paralyzed by my own fear. I then get confronted by an inner counter-position that can be so dominating that it blocks my original impulse to take up a counter-attack position. Here too we notice the close relationship between positioning and being positioned, a process that takes place not only between people but also within our own inner make-up. What happens between individuals reflects what takes place inside our inner selves. These two processes jointly determine the actual behavior of people in relation to their social environment.

The Role of the Other within Yourself

The advantage of the concept of *I*-position is that we can involve the other person in our own self-esteem and in our self-narrative. It means that another person can function as an *I*-position in your own self. Here is an example: At a very young age we are so involved with our parents or our teachers that they assume a position in our own selves. The same process happens with family members, friends, colleagues, and new acquaintances. You can have the feeling that at certain moments you act like your father, your mother, your sister, brother, or girlfriend. The other person enters into the center of your own universe. Sometimes you can even feel what another significant person is feeling. Sometimes you will notice: "I now talk just like my father." It can happen that a counter-response arises immediately: "But I only want to be different and react differently!" This is the dynamic interplay of position and counter-position. To establish your own identity, it is necessary that you differentiate your own *I*-position from the *I*-position of the other person in yourself. Just think how one of your parents can be so dominant in the organization of your inner make-up that you do not know if it is you yourself who wants something, or the mother-in-yourself or the father-in yourself who wants it. Some people choose a career or study that seems to originate in their own selves, but later they come to realize that the choice they made was determined more by an external position that was interiorized in themselves, than from an *I*-position that occurred within their own autonomy. In that case a learning process is required to make a distinction between the other-in-myself and the position you take as I-myself.

For our own personal development, it is good to realize that we are not just completely isolated individuals, but that the other is simultaneously living in ourselves. This can happen in a very positive way. Just think about people who we greatly admire or who function as models: A family member, a person of the

FIGURE 1.2 Others as external *I*-positions in ourselves
Drawing by Diederik Grootjans (reproduced with permission)

8 Part 1 Opposition

stature of a Mandela[1] or Malala Yousafzai[2], an inspiring teacher, or a pop star. In the theory of this book we consider a significant other as "another I." This was established long ago by the Greek philosopher Aristotle: In his book *Nicomachean ethics* (Pakaluk, 2005), dedicated to his son, he proposed that you develop the highest level of a relationship with another person when you consider the other as an "alter ego." In the other person you recognize yourself (*ego*) while at the same time you acknowledge them as someone who is different from you (*alter*). If you can understand this idea and are able to experience it, then, according to Aristotle, you achieve the highest form of friendship.

Summarizing

- An *I*-position refers to the way in which you position yourself in relation to other people and yourself.
- We can assume multiple *I*-positions that are inter-related to each other. Also, one position can, at different times, be more dominant in the self than the others.
- We not only position ourselves, but we get positioned by others as well.
- As a response to being positioned by other persons, we can invoke a counter-position in ourselves and therefore we will never be fully determined as positioned by the other person.
- The other person can function as an *I*-position in our own self. Ideally, the other functions as an alter ego. We recognize ourselves (*ego*) in the other, but at the same time we also realize that this person is different from us (*alter*).

Critical questions

The theory we describe here is an invitation to you to use it as a "lens" through which to look at yourself in a new way, and to consider how this might influence your interaction with other individuals. The questions "Who am I?" or "What is my identity?" get answered by the claim that you don't have only *one* identity, but multiple different identities in the form of *I*-positions that are different and even contradictory. This is not a static view of the self, but a dynamic process of positioning and counter-positioning.

- What do you think of this proposition? What reasons would you give to convince other people that you have only *one* identity, or conversely that you have different and multiple identities, without being "schizophrenic"?
- Can you find in the text parts that, according to you, do not cover the subjects or are not completely accurate? Can you say in your own words what you think is missing? How would you argue against it? And what reasons can you give for that point of view?

- Have you ever experienced that another person is functioning as part of yourself? In the text we mention that this can occur through the presence of the other person in yourself (e.g., "my father in myself"). Do you think this statement is correct, or do you think other factors might play a role? How can we find out what those factors are?

Exercise

I-positions and counter-positions arise in the interaction with other people, people with whom we have different kinds of interactions. *I*-positions can also relate to a position you occupy in society, the role you play in it. We all are citizens of a country, but we are also consumers, and many of us are also students, or employees. So for most of us additional *I*-positions exist, depending on the roles you play in society. Can you describe some of your own *I*-positions? These *I*-positions do not have to be compatible. As a consumer and as a citizen you have different interests, desires, preferences, etc. Most of the time we do not notice this immediately, because we are positioned in one role or the other. But we notice that different positions and counter-positions can occur. For example, there may be no single political party that completely embodies what you yourself find important. As a citizen you choose a certain political party, but that doesn't mean that in other situations, or at other moments you might have a different counter-position toward that same party.

- Choose two *I*-positions, for example, "I as citizen" and "I as consumer". Brainstorm[3] what values you find important for yourself as a citizen. After that, do the same for yourself as a consumer.

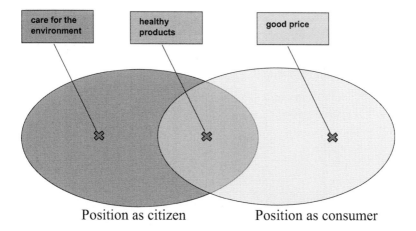

FIGURE 1.3 Venn diagram

10 Part 1 Opposition

- Look at the remarks you have written down to see if you think they relate to things you considered as valuable for that position.
- Put the positions in a Venn diagram, as shown in Figure 1.3
- Do the positions overlap and is there a huge overlap, or none at all?
- Where do you notice the differences in the positions?
- Can you initiate a conversation between your position as a citizen and your position as a consumer? Can you describe the character of that conversation?

Reflecting

- Look back at the situation you described in "From Your Own Experience" at the start of this chapter. You referred to a situation in which you were in a relationship with other individuals.
- Do you now observe different I-positions in yourself? Can you describe them?
- Do you also recognize I-positions in other persons? What role do you play in establishing I-positions or counter-positions in other individuals? What is your influence on certain positions in other individuals?
- What other questions do you have about this subject?

Notes

1. Nelson Mandela (1918–2013) was an iconic fighter against apartheid and became president of the Republic of South Africa after more than 20 years in prison. He has been an inspirational figure to people around the world, especially to those who make a case for racial justice and equality.
2. Malala Yousafzai is a Pakistani activist for female education. In 2012 she was shot by a Taliban gunman in an assassination attempt in retaliation for her activism. In 2014, she was the co-recipient of the Nobel Peace Prize, and the youngest ever recipient.
3. When brainstorming, you want to come up with as many ideas and viewpoints as possible that could be answers to the question. While in the brainstorming phase, try not to figure out if the ideas are correct or not. After the brainstorming, when you think you have contributed enough ideas, check which ones are the most useful.

2

ARE YOU TOLERANT OF ALTERNATIVE VIEWPOINTS?

How do we relate to the points of view and opinions of others? Why do we prefer so strongly to "be right" and to be in the company of people who share the same points of view? In this chapter we focus on the development of a position that makes it possible to have a democratic dialogue with other people who differ from us in their opinions on certain issues.

From Your Own Experience

You probably are familiar with the term "bubble" or "echo-chamber." Most writers and journalists agree that we all live in bubbles—groups of people who agree with each other, share the same opinions, and communicate easily with each other—but we don't behave in the same way when we are in the company of people who have completely different opinions. Many people don't like to sit at the dinner table when that obstinate uncle with his weird political ideas is also present. And it's difficult to interact with a person who never stops commenting and criticizing.[1]

What about your own bubble? Do you, too, live in a bubble? How does that bubble look to you? What are the most important characteristics of your bubble? When answering these questions, you don't just have to concentrate on opinions. You can also consider your level of education, life-style habits, consumption, music preferences, etc. Do you deny that you yourself live in a bubble? That is possible, but can you explain why it is plausible? Try it! Also, do you know people in your social environment who entertain vastly different opinions and feelings about viewpoints and considerations that are very important to you? Write down what is your own bubble, or your thoughts about it.

12 Part 1 Opposition

Background Information

Assuming Alternative Points of View

In our daily lives, we naturally adopt points of view that are different from those of others: "I think that…," "I cannot agree with that…," "I am convinced that…," "That's nonsense," "My view is that…." Formulated differently: we always assume certain positions, and once we have formulated them we are inclined to stick to them. This is something very remarkable. Once we have formed an opinion or assumed a point of view, we are inclined to put a shell around it so we can protect that opinion or conviction from alternative views, and certainly from convictions that are in conflict with ours. Once we have formed an opinion, we automatically put a defensive wall around it and then the original conviction or opinion, certainly in its more advanced phases, is hard to change. That is why alternative points of view that deviate from an original standpoint have little or no chance to permeate our system of convictions. Exactly because they are considered as undermining our own opinions, other convictions or viewpoints get pushed aside and will be ignored. The possible *rationale* or gain that is contained in those alternative convictions will not be given the opportunity to penetrate our mind. They get firmly locked out, ignored, or simply referred to as "nonsense."

Consistent Identity and the Valuable Feeling of Self-Esteem

Why do we have the inclination to firmly stick to a previously held position? The answer is: We need opinions and viewpoints because they give us support in a world that is vastly chaotic. Suppose we allow ourselves to be influenced by all opinions that we are confronted with, and adhere to them without any resistance or critical assessment. Then we are like a leaf that floats in the wind with no sense of direction or purpose. Then no stability can be found in our actions and behavior, and we would end up in a chaotic situation. But we all have the feeling that we are the same person we were yesterday and that we have the same identity over time. To assume a certain point of view gives a sense of continuity to our lives and contributes to our feeling of identity, as William James (1890) emphasized.

Moreover, when we cherish a certain point of view we retain a feeling of self-esteem. Research has shown that holding on to an unwavering point of view might be helpful in covering up underlying feelings of uncertainty (McGregor & Marigold, 2003). When other people acknowledge and admire a certain point of view that you are expressing, this might contribute to your own feeling of self-esteem: This is where I stand and this is who I am. That's why it is understandable that people feel attracted to acquaintances, friends, and groups who share their own cherished attitudes and views. This has the virtue that your self-esteem receives a positive boost over and over again. But the disadvantage is that you will not learn something new or get to know alternative points of view, something that might be valuable to yourself as a person and as a participant in society. When you stick to your own opinions and are not willing to seriously consider alternative opinions and viewpoints, you run the risk that you will be locked up in your own bubble. We notice this in the frequent use of "likes" on Facebook and other social media. The more "likes" you get, the better. But acquiring more knowledge about a certain subject is not equivalent to boosting your self-esteem. You might feel comfortable when someone is repeatedly patting you on the back, but you run the risk that you are not using your own judgment in making the right choices in everyday life. After all, you learn more from people who disagree with you in a constructive way, than from people who just confirm your current points of view.

This self-affirmative effect can be noticed too in the formation of group cultures. People seek contact with groups with which they can identify themselves, and then they start to pick up the same thought processes or ideologies as the other members of the group. In social psychology this phenomenon is known as "groupthink" (Gastil, 1994). This way of thinking occurs when the desire for mutual harmony is so strong that critical evaluation is absent, and alternative viewpoints are not taken into account. This happens when members of a group, driven by loyalty to their own group, avoid conflicts, reject deviant opinions, and isolate themselves from perspectives that are incompatible with those of the group. The views of other people and other groups will then be devalued or ignored with disdain. People then envelop themselves in their own bubble or, as described often, they stay in the echo chamber of their own rightness. But in between staying comfortably in one's own echo chamber, and getting annoyed by people who are always criticizing and disagreeing with us (flame wars),[2] lies a "valley of open-mindedness" where productive discussions can take place (Figure 2.1). To better understand how this valley of open-mindedness works, we need some insight into the boundaries of *I*-positions.

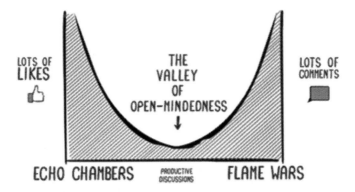

FIGURE 2.1 Valley of open-mindedness
Source: Wikimedia Commons

14 Part 1 Opposition

HONG KONG, CHINA, AND THE LACK OF OPEN-MINDEDNESS

Open-mindedness is not only a possibility of the mind of individual people, but its presence or absence can also be observed at the level of states. A contemporary example is the relationship between Hong Kong and China during the 2019 Hong Kong uproar. While China is striving for one united state, Hong Kong is claiming its relative political independence and defends its democratic rights against the autocratically led giant. China could not prevent part of its territory falling prey to a violent anarchy that undermines the political pretensions of the superpower. Universities became battlefields and demonstrating students were attacking the police with Molotov cocktails. This upsurge was a clash between Hong Kong students' claim of political independence, as expressed in the slogan "Free Hong Kong, revolution now," and president Xi Jinping's autocratically led state, which has become more authoritarian since he came to power. As Financial Times commentator Gideon Rachman (2019) argues, the situation is highly precarious because the Hong Kong rebellion undermines the central principle of the patriotic education that makes a strong case for one China, one that brings together all citizens as united in one centrally governed state. Many Hong Kong citizens, however, prefer a strong Hong Kong identity leading to a chasm between its democratic aspirations and the Chinese ideal of undivided unity. Rachman concludes that it is almost impossible for President Xi to find a way to give an appropriate response to this polarizing situation, because the political system lacks the open-mindedness and tolerance to create space for alternative points of view and possibilities. This results in a political situation in which the positions are closed, and even rigid, on both sides of the conflict.

Boundaries of I-positions: Open or Closed

What happens when we look at the concept of open-mindedness through the lens of *I*-positions? We need to take into consideration that those positions have boundaries that can be open or closed. To understand the process of positioning, we need to look at this phenomenon from a rather nuanced point of view, as Brown (2006) has suggested.

If the boundaries of a position are OPEN, we are able to look beyond the limits of our own point of view and we can consider alternative or even contrary opinions. In doing so, one can be receptive towards a person who holds a viewpoint that is completely new or alien to your own. You can then become empathic toward the positions and feelings of your partner in a dialogue. (This is important for the concept of "empathy" that we will address in later chapters of the book.)

But holding an open position can become so open that it becomes overridden by a contrary position. That happens when the boundaries of your own position are very SOFT, with the consequence that closing the boundary becomes extremely difficult, or is even no longer possible. We observe this phenomenon when we see a person behave in a rather over-dependent way towards another individual. This is what we also characterize as a symbiotic relationship. If you are part of a symbiotic relationship, then it is very difficult to rely on your own judgment when you have to make important decisions, or when you are faced with a difficult decision.

The boundaries of a position can also be CLOSED. Closing boundaries is necessary if somebody tries to exploit you and is all too eager to make use of your willingness to help them. When you position yourself as willing to be helpful, but the other person sees you as someone who is "always there for them" when they need you, then the result is that they always can and might overstep your boundaries. In situations where you might need to protect yourself and have to yell "stop!" it is very important that you are able to close the boundaries around your own position.

But a closed-off position can deteriorate into a position with RIGID boundaries. Someone who stands ready to defend themselves when they encounter the slightest contradiction or conflict can find themselves immediately threatened, and then act in a possibly permanently defensive way by closing themselves off in a position with rigid boundaries. Such a person occupies a closed position, no matter the nature of a specific situation. The closing of the boundaries then becomes structural by ignoring the specific nature of the situation. In an extreme version, we can see this behavior displayed in people with a paranoid mindset. They are afraid of revealing thoughts that can be used against them. And even when other people show good intentions, they might come to believe that they detect hidden threats in what other people say or do. As a counter-reaction, they might develop a position with rigid boundaries.

By using these distinctions, we can formulate an important prerequisite for allowing alternative points of view. We can summarize this as follows: To admit alternative viewpoints, a FLEXIBLE position-repertoire is required. In such a repertoire, we encounter positions that are *open* enough to allow alternatives. Examples of open positions are: "I as interested in the viewpoints of other people," "I as explorative," and "I as trying to understand what happens there," meaning that I really like to learn something I didn't know before. However, these positions should not to be too *soft* because that would prevent taking up a position that is contrary to a rival position. The position-repertoire should also contain positions that are firm enough to formulate your own viewpoint and clarify it to other people and yourself ("I'm not letting anybody walk over me," "I resist when it's needed"). But the boundaries of the positions may not become too *rigid* so that you become defensive and distrustful toward people with

16 Part 1 Opposition

alternative points of view. Flexibility of the position-repertoire implies that, depending on the specific situation, you are able to switch from open to closed positions, and vice versa. A flexible position repertoire helps you to arrive, stay, or return to the valley of open-mindedness. As the old saying goes: "A mind is like a parachute. It does not work if it is not open."[3]

Summarizing

- We need opinions and viewpoints to hold ourselves together in an otherwise fragmented and often chaotic world.
- Opinions and viewpoints contribute to an identity that becomes reasonably stabilized over time and will give us a feeling of self-esteem.
- However, it becomes problematic if we stay in our own bubble and no longer exhibit tolerance for alternative viewpoints.
- To understand this process, we need to keep our eyes and minds open to the boundaries of the positions we ourselves occupy. Those boundaries can be open (we admit other positions as our own) or closed (we take a firm position when a certain situation asks for it). In a problematic case those positions may be soft (susceptible to multiple kinds of opinions) or rigid (feeling threatened and always being on the defensive).
- Ideally, we might develop a flexible position-repertoire that, depending on the specific ramifications of the situation, helps us to assume an open or closed position so that we can enter the valley of open-mindedness.

Critical Questions

In the text, we examined the argument that taking up a point of view, or clearly voicing your own opinion, contributes to the feeling that you yourself over time stay the same person. Is that really the case? Do you recognize this in yourself? And if it also contributes to your feeling of self-esteem, do you then feel that other people are supportive of your behavior?

What do you think about some of the statements made in the text? Are there arguments you question? Try to formulate your questions very precisely. Discuss your questions with your classmates: How do you find an answer?

Exercise

To have a discussion with other people in a democracy at large you need to use a flexible position-repertoire. This means that you might start a conversation with other people from a firm position (i.e., a reasonably closed one), in which you defend your own point of view. Otherwise, you might run the risk of being seen as a leaf that is blown with the wind. At the same time, your own position also needs to be sufficiently open to take into account the views of other people. You can practice this. We will first describe the exercise, then give an example to clarify how the exercise functions.

Formulate an opinion about an actual issue. Choose an issue that is important to you. We recommend that you formulate your point of view in a short sentence.

- What are the personal values that support your point of view?
- And then ask yourself what reasons you have for this point of view. Write those down.

Suppose now that you want to start a conversation with someone who has made it clear that they hold a very different opinion about this subject.

- How solid is your position in your initial conversation? Would you consider other perspectives? And if so, which are those?
- Is there also an open position in you? Can you change or adapt your initial firmly held position? How do you characterize that position?

Example to Clarify the Exercise

We have to change radically to sun and wind energy to halt climate change.

- **Values**: Good and healthy life climate for all people on Earth; the survival of all species.
- **Reasons**: It is necessary to reduce CO_2 emissions and increase sustainable energy.
- **A closed position**: Everybody should reduce energy consumption by 15 percent starting next year.
- **An open position**: Allow other possibilities by also taking economic aspects into consideration.

Reflecting

- Do you remember what we discussed in Chapter 1? (No, don't surreptitiously look back to the chapter).
- Can you already detect different *I*-positions in yourself? Can you name some of them?
- Which of those positions would you label as open? And which as closed?
- In general, in which situations are you able to communicate with a flexible position-repertoire?

18 Part 1 Opposition

- Go back to what you said in "From Your Own Experience" at the start of this chapter. You wrote down there what is your own bubble, and your thoughts about it. Has this changed, or remained the same? If it has changed, what do you think is the main reason? If it has not changed, can you give reasons for this?

Notes

1. Here is a very useful website when your angry, always disagreeing uncle wants to talk about politics. What do you do? https://www.nytimes.com/interactive/2019/11/26/opinion/family-holiday-talk-impeachment.html
2. A flame war is a lengthy exchange of angry or abusive messages, typically between users of an online forum.
3. Goodreads, read January, 22, 2020.

3

SUSPENSION OF JUDGMENT

Why is it So Difficult?

When we give quick and hasty responses in a conversation, sometimes our immediate reaction is "What nonsense!" In this way we close ourselves off from what the other person is saying. What other answers can we give? How can we deal with our initial impulsive responses in a reasonable way? This is where the concept of suspension of judgment comes into play.

From Your Own Experience

Have you ever had the experience when you made a suggestion or vented your opinion about something, and someone else rejected your suggestion or let you know immediately in no uncertain terms—before you even could finish your sentence—that they disagreed with you?

How did you respond to that situation? Did it annoy you? Did it make you feel insecure? Irritated? Did you stop talking? Or … ?

Or is this something you have not experienced very often? Could it be that it you are the one who interrupts other people? Could it be that you are not giving other people enough space to express their own opinions?

Do you immediately state your own point of view? Or are you willing to listen to someone else's responses before you express your own view?

Can you write down some of your impressions as answers to these questions?

Background Information

Developing your inner democracy requires that you are able to listen attentively to other people as well as to yourself. But that doesn't occur automatically. You might ask yourself: Why not? In our conversations with other people, something gets

20 Part 1 Opposition

triggered in us, a thought or emotion that temporarily fights for priority. We then become influenced not only by what another person says or does, but also by our own feelings and thoughts, which might conflict with what another person is saying. Listening carefully to someone else and responding in an appropriate way requires a "suspension of judgment." What do we mean by that?

One of the most influential researchers who carried out fundamental work on suspension of judgment is the physicist David Bohm (1996). He became well-known for his book *On dialogue*, in which he thoroughly and systematically researched the process of dialogue between people, with an emphasis on the value of listening. He assembled people in groups who communicated with each other without an agenda, and then he studied the processes that took place. He discovered that a fruitful dialogue is only possible when you choose to put your own opinions on the backburner, rather than immediately verbalizing them. This is, of course, easier said than done. According to Bohm's theory, there are two responses that one should *not* give in a dialogical conversation. First, suppose you hear a statement that you think is nonsense, and your spontaneous response is: "This is ridiculous" or "This is absurd." To openly *express* yourself in this way is not very productive because it is painful for your partner in the conversation. The chances are great that your conversation partners will close themselves off and no longer want to freely talk about certain issues. (In this context, we remind you about the closing of boundaries of a previously held position that we discussed earlier). It is also unproductive because you yourself are no longer open to the position of the other person and also no longer open to enriching your own ideas with the ideas of others' positions. The second, similarly undesirable approach is to strongly control yourself and *suppress* the expression of spontaneous responses so that your ideas cannot be shared.

Both reactions—blindly following your impulse or repressing it—are counter-productive if what you want is to really listen to your partner in a dialogical conversation. Suspension of judgment requires that in a communication with another person, you devote *attention* to what is going on in another person and in yourself. You accomplish this by delaying your response—by not immediately and unreflectively expressing your first thoughts or feelings about an issue.

Paying Attention to Emotional Responses

Suspension of judgment implies that you give time and attention not only to what is going on in the mind of another person, but also to what is taking place within your own self. And for this to happen, it is important that you pay attention to the emotional responses of the other person as well as yourself. You will become aware of these emotional responses if you pay close attention to them. If another person expresses something, then it is helpful when you are not solely focused on their literal verbal expressions, but also take in their non-verbal body language and facial expressions. You might then notice the angry expression on the face of the other person, the deep frown between their eyebrows, the way their lips are pressed together. It can even happen that people suddenly start to smile at an emotional moment. What is lurking behind that smile or frown? Anger? Frustration? Irritation? Surprise?

When we want to learn how to suspend our judgment, according to Bohm it is essential that we also pay attention to our own emotions. We often do not pay attention to this element in the conversation because we are focused on what our partner in the conversation is saying, and we are already formulating what we ourselves want to say before our conversation partners are finished with their remarks. The result is that we spend more time and energy on our own thought processes than on those of other people. This all takes place in a very brief time frame, and it happens almost automatically. Noticing how you physically respond to your partner in a conversation is essential for suspension of judgment. Suppose another person is saying something that you consider repulsive. If you pay attention to your own non-verbal expressions you will notice that you can become internally cramped, your throat gets tightened, your muscles are tensing, you are breathing more heavily and you are clenching your fists, all signs that you are now adopting a "closed position." Suspension of judgment requires that you do not just respond from that cramped and closed position, but that you also pay attention to these emotions. During that moment of attention, you are creating space and time to not just follow your first impulse, but to come up with a different response. Instead of quickly and impulsively saying "What a stupid idea" or "Absurd," you might say "I notice that this touches me" or " I have to think more about this" or "Could it be also the case that ... ."

Researchers interested in how group processes work have developed guidelines that are helpful for the suspension of judgment (Burson, 2002). Two of those guidelines are very important:

- *listening* without immediately giving a response
- showing *respect* by asking questions for clarification.

To develop inner democracy, these guidelines are also important in the relations people have towards their own self. You listen to your own remarks and those of your partner in the conversation, and you also pay attention to non-verbal reactions and signals. Instead of denying your psychological and bodily responses, you treat them with respect and as sources of information about what is going on between you and the other person. Giving careful attention to your own responses, even if you do not consider them adequate or supportive, might be helpful in suspending your judgment.

22 Part 1 Opposition

Understanding Instead of Opinionating

Listening attentively and showing respect is difficult when we are immediately inclined to give priority to our own opinions. The problem here is that we often give an opinion before we have thought carefully about the subject, and before we have consulted ourselves to see if our opinion makes sense. So it makes sense to replace the question "What do I think about this?" with "How can I make sense of this?" This is called withholding your immediate opinion. You first ask yourself: Do I have enough knowledge about this? Do I understand it sufficiently? And then, only later, you can try to formulate an opinion, albeit in a very careful and appropriate manner.

Summarizing

The following points are important for understanding what we mean by the concept of suspension of judgment.

- Both expressing an opinion unreflectively, and suppressing an opinion, are non-productive forms of behavior.
- In a conversation with someone else, it makes sense to pay attention to the other person's body language, as well as your own bodily and inner responses.
- Listening carefully and showing respect by asking clarifying questions are essential requirements in this process.
- Listening and showing respect promotes this process by replacing the question "What is my opinion about this?" with the question "How might I better understand this?"

Critical questions

- Do you think that in the previous text the importance of "suspension of judgment" is sufficiently clear to you?
- The immediate and direct expression of an opinion such as "What nonsense!" is described as unproductive. Do you agree with that? Such statements are surely very clear … or maybe not?
- In the text it is also emphasized that you have to pay attention to the other person's emotions as well as your own. Why is this so important? After all, you can just listen to what another person has to say about a certain issue in a passive way.
- Are there any other questions you have about the text? Try to formulate them in a precise way. Discuss your questions with other participants in your group.

Exercises

Exercise 1

A triangular relation

The first exercise involves three people. There are three roles. The first role is the narrator, the second the questioner, and the third the observer. This exercise takes 5 minutes, and afterwards you are going to discuss the observer's reactions.

The **narrator** makes remarks about something that has happened recently, a short time ago. You give your most sincere opinion. You can choose a situation or event that has happened to you. You can also choose a subject in the news, something that other people might also have heard. But choose something that touches you, something that made you upset, sad, or happy. Describe the situation briefly and then summarize your opinion in a short statement.

In the next five minutes the **questioner** will ask questions of the narrator, but not give any judgment. You can only ask questions for clarification, such as: "What do you mean by ... ?"; "Do I understand you correctly when you say ... ." Halfway, and again at the end of the session, the questioner summarizes what they think the narrator was expressing and on what grounds (the observer gives you a sign). You should use the same words as the narrator as much as possible. This means, try not to formulate the narrative only in your own words. Your most important task is to listen carefully to the narrator, and not let them detect what you think of their opinion.

The **observer** monitors both the narrator and the questioner. What do you observe in their body language and facial expressions? How do you interpret them? Do you perceive underlying emotions? Pay attention also to the time frame for this part of the exercise, and ask the questioner to give a summary halfway and shortly before the end of the session.

After five minutes, both narrator and questioner discuss their experiences in response to the observer's remarks. Crucial to this follow-up discussion is the question of how emotions have played a positive or negative role for the narrator.

We recommend repeating this exercise at least once more, with everyone in the group assuming a different role than before. That way you can elevate the practice to a higher level.

- Has the suspension of judgment contributed to the quality of the conversation?
- Were the summaries and questions provided by the questioner helpful?
- Has the questioner merely suspended his or her judgment, or just not showed it in an open and direct way?
- Can the questioner observe the non-verbal and other facial expressions of the narrator, and do they refer to them in their questioning and in their summary?

24 Part 1 Opposition

FIGURE 3.1 Photo from Unsplash

Exercise 2

Can you see it differently?

What do you see in this picture?

Can you describe what you see in this picture, without giving value judgments, opinions, etc. If you think you can do so, is your description of the picture still a judgment or not? OR: Why is it hard to describe this picture without expressing any value judgments?

You can't describe a picture (certainly not a picture such as this one) without interpreting what you see. The picture tells you a story in a certain way, and that story has an impact on you. Try to formulate a completely different story about this picture, one that is still plausible (to help you out a little bit: what is this picture not showing?).

Reflecting

- Return to what you have written down under "From Your Own Experience." There you reflected on whether you are inclined to give an impulsive and immediate response to a conversation partner.
- In this chapter we have considered the importance of suspending your judgment, and we did some exercises on that. Think about future situations in which you are challenged to wait before giving your impulsive response. In particular, take into account what you have learned in Exercise 2.
- Can you give different interpretations of the picture in Exercise 3? What does this insight mean to you? Compare it with a situation where you immediately assume that you know what is happening.

4

FLEXIBLE CHANGE OF PERSPECTIVE

Be flexible like a dancer

The position from which we view reality reveals just a tiny part of that reality. The world around us, and other people, show different aspects if we look at them from various and different points of view. This is what we mean when we address the topic of changing perspective. In this chapter we are challenging you to see if you are able to change your perspective regarding a particular topic.

From Your Own Experience

First, let's think about someone you know very well. Write down their name. Which different *I*-position do you use when you describe that person? Write those down next to their name. And which of their *I*-positions are you not really certain of or familiar with? Write those down too. It is difficult to describe *I*-positions that you are not familiar with. Can you still say that you know this person, even though you do not know them in all their *I*-positions? Why do you think that is the case?

Background Information

If we have an opinion or a judgment about something, then we seem to be doing this from a certain perspective. It is not really possible to see the reality only from *one* certain perspective. Suppose you see a beautiful church and you are standing there, looking at the façade with admiration. But does this mean that you really "see" the church in its entirety? If you have seen this church from the front, then you don't know what the back side of the building looks like. But by walking around the church, you will see it from different perspectives. And you will get

26 Part 1 Opposition

to know the church even better once you go inside. Then you will notice many more new things. By walking around the building and by walking from the outside to the inside, you will gradually get to know much more about the church. But you have to merge those diverse perspectives into an overall picture. This re-construction gives you a picture of how the church looks to you. This principle, looking at something from different perspectives and making a composition of them, is something we can also apply in our relationships with other people. You get to know someone better if you perceive them from several different perspectives, instead of just *one*. Suppose you meet someone in a bar or at a party. You get a first impression of that person, but at that moment you have no idea how they will behave in other situations: on a sports field, in a study group, or with their loved ones. You can only form a complete picture of someone when you encounter them in different situations that give you the opportunity to get to know them from different angles. The different situations offer you different perspectives. This requires that you can *change* and adjust your perspectives, and eventually *combine* those perspectives in order to construct a coherent impression of the other person.

But we can take this one step further. Just as in the example of the church, you can also try to enter the experiential world of a person in order to get to know their inner self. You then get to know the other person by assuming their positions. Positioning yourself into the several positions of another person gives you a glance at the inner world of that person. In this way, you get a broader array of perspectives, from which you come to learn more about the other.

Taking the position of the other requires empathy. Here is the fundamental question: What makes it possible to not only know the positions of another individual but also to experience their underlying emotions and feelings? Only when we can assume the position of someone else's experiences and their feelings, can we speak of empathy. It allows us to assume the perspective of the other. When empathy is not present, it is not really possible to understand another person and communicate with them. We then stay strangers to each other (we will go more deeply into the concept of empathy in Chapter 13).

The emotional component of empathy is essential for getting to know someone else. This means that you will get to know the other person *from the inside* so that you get to know them more profoundly and intimately. You might ask yourself: Yes, I might very well express certain things, but how might the other person experience this? Or you might think: If I try to put myself in their position, then I might realize that I should say things differently. If we hurt other people's feelings, it often happens because we intentionally or unintentionally do not consider the feelings we evoke in others as a consequence of our own expressions or actions.

Changing Perspective: The Three-Step Model

The three-step scientific model (Hermans & Hermans-Konopka, 2010, originally proposed by Marková, 1987) might be useful for understanding the flexible changing of perspectives. This model illustrates how you can develop a counter-position that is different from the one you had assumed originally. The model consists of three steps.

Step 1: I have an opinion and I express this to another person.
Step 2: The other person listens to this opinion and responds to it.
Step 3: I come back to my original opinion and reconsider it by interweaving elements of the response of the other participant.

Let's look at this from the perspective of someone who is concerned about the many immigrants who come into their country.

Step 1: I think it's a problem that so many immigrants come to my country. Our country is already full!
Step 2: My conversation partner objects to my line of thought by saying: "I understand your concerns. But if you count the number of immigrants who enter our country, then you also have to count the many immigrants who leave the country."
Step 3: Yes fine, but I still think there is an immigration problem. However, I do have to consider the many people who leave this country.

This example shows that after the response from my conversation partner, I am not repeating my original point of view in the same way (Our country is already full), but I reconsider my initial statement and give a more nuanced version by considering the expressions from my partner in the conversation. In so doing I assume a re-positioning of my original view and I am not just giving a repeated version of my opinion. And this is what is happening: after having reviewed my original opinion and after comparing it with other opinions, I am beginning to develop my original position in a different direction.

This re-positioning of an original point of view is not in itself self-evident. People who speak and think from a strongly negative interpretation or framework regarding their view of the world, find it hard to change their positions. Think about people who are inclined to react from a rather defensive or suspicious perspective. Thus, when another person gives a certain opinion, then this might be considered as a critique or an attack. Even when someone says something nice and friendly, this might be interpreted in a negative way. Certain individuals might then think: The other person needs something from me, and therefore they say something nice because they want something from me. In this

FIGURE 4.1 Changing your *I*-position needs a flexible mind
Source: Wikimedia Commons

case, the person is reacting from an *I*-position (e.g., I as threatened) that can be so dominating that it is impossible for them to assume another position. They feel threatened by all contradictions and oppositions and then withdraw behind the walls of a rigid position. In this case, the person will not be able to re-consider their original point of view. For example, when they say at step 1: "People are evil" and another person contradicts them, then the first person will only cling to their original viewpoint and not acknowledge the arguments of the other party.

Let's summarize this: To facilitate a change of perspective, it is necessary that you temporarily leave behind your own position and frame of mind and consider the position of the other person, and do this in an empathic way. You can express your original point of view to your conversation partner, and after listening to their response you might want to change your original point of view.

What Does it Mean to "Hold On Firmly to Your Own Opinion"?

The following statement is ascribed to the French philosopher Voltaire (1694–1778): "Opinions have caused more ills than the plague or earthquakes on this little globe of ours." No doubt this Enlightment thinker and early advocate of human rights was referring to opinions whereby people suppress each other and are even willing to destroy each other. In other words, harmful opinions might originate typically from advocating rigid and unwavering positions.

That is why it is wise to keep in mind an expression that is ascribed to Plato: "Opinion is the medium between knowledge and ignorance." This striking insight shows us that we surely know *something*, but if we think that we know *it*, then we are on the path to a risky ignorance of which we are not aware. Plato's insight shows us that an opinion is a starting point but not an end point. It is a starting point if it is open enough to become influenced by the opinions or viewpoints of others and to permit contradictions in ourselves. To put it differently, an opinion is always a provisional point of view that asks for a clarification and leaves room for constructive contradiction. Precisely because of this contradiction, an opinion can be confirmed, disputed, or developed further. An opinion can have potential only if it also embraces a question: Is this correct? Can it be this way? Is there another side to this case? With complex issues there are always more and other sides to consider.

Forming an opinion is ultimately a social process—it is a little ripple in the stream of various other opinions that can invalidate, supplement, or enrich our own opinion. Well-known expressions such as "We all live in the bubbles of our own rightness" and "We get locked into our own echo chambers" all lead to questions of how we form opinions in the public domain. By bursting these bubbles, we come to realize that opinions are only fruitful for society at large if they originate from open positions that tolerate contradiction and opposition. Permitting and observing contradiction and allowing opposition is what lies at the core of democracy at large and, more importantly, at the heart of our own inner democracy.

Summarizing

- To obtain a flexible change in perspective requires perceiving something or somebody from different perspectives, even contrary ones.
- To accomplish this, empathy is needed because it facilitates getting in touch with the inner thoughts and feelings of another person.
- The three-step model is useful for incorporating the responses of the other person in your own opinion. (This doesn't necessarily mean that you have to give up your own point of view.)
- Your own opinion is a starting point, not an end point, and it awaits a response from yourself or from other people.

30 Part 1 Opposition

Critical Questions

- In the text, we suggested that you can only form an accurate picture of someone else when you experience that person in different situations, meaning you get to know that person from various perspectives. How does this relate to what you wrote down earlier in the section "From Your Own Experience"?
- In the text, we mentioned that having an opinion functions as a starting point. How do you understand that statement? What do you think it means?
- Are there elements in the text that puzzle you and that you perhaps do not fully understand? You can discuss these diverse viewpoints with the participants in your group.

Exercise

In the text, we presented the three-step model.

Step 1: I assume a point of view on some topic and express this to someone else.
Step 2: The other person listens to this point of view and responds to it.
Step 3: I return to my original point of view and then start to revise this viewpoint by incorporating some elements of the other person's responses.

When there are just two of you, you can easily do this exercise. Follow each of the three steps. You assume a certain position on a topic, the other person listens and responds, and subsequently you incorporate this response into your own point of view. Do this twice so that each of you has the experience of what it means to assume a certain position and respond to a different point of view.

Now you ask other people to participate in this exercise. Question: How would you look at this topic from the perspective of other people, and to which other opinions might this lead? Start with the person you chose in at the start of this chapter, under "From Your Own Experience," and try to imagine how this person would look at the selected topic. Then choose another person and imagine their perspective. Can you now reconsider your own opinions in light of the three-step model we have discussed?

Example to Clarify the Exercise

Maybe this exercise needs some clarification. We started with the premise that our country is full! You can hold this opinion from a certain *I*-position, such as "I as a safety-seeking person." I am a teacher (in education). I have got to know children of refugees, and I don't think they should be sent back to the countries from which they came. But I am also a person who lives in a particular neighborhood, and from this standpoint I can formulate anew another position.

What this shows is that, first of all, you need to have access to your different *I*-positions to start a dialogue about those different points of view. Then you invite other people into the discussion. How would you look at these issues from the perspective of several different people, and what would the outcome be? Think, for example, about an employer in the agricultural industry, a manager in a supermarket, an unemployed person, or someone with immigrant parents who was born in your country. When you place yourself in the shoes of such a person, would you, more or less, be willing to modify your initial position on the chosen topic?

Reflecting

- In Exercise 2, we have tried to take on flexible positions according to the three-step model, first with a co-student, then with different *I*-positions in yourself, and finally with the *I*-positions of another person. Make a note of the parts in the exercise that you found difficult and those that you consider as easy.
- Write down what you have learned about other people's perspectives. In particular, think about what wrote about the person you selected at the start, under "From Your Own Experience."

5

META-POSITIONS

Look at Yourself as if from a Helicopter in the Sky

In Chapter 4, we wanted to show how important it is to view the world around us from different perspectives. In this chapter, we return to our different *I*-positions and try to find a perspective from which we can oversee our various *I*-positions clearly, and connect them with each other. We will introduce you to a new concept that you may not be familiar with, but that is helpful in getting some *overview* of your present thoughts: Assuming a meta-position.

From Your Own Experience

In Chapter 1 we saw that we all have different *I*-positions, for example, "I as a citizen" and "I as a consumer." There are similarities among these positions, but they can also be very different from each other. We do not necessarily recognize in each of these *I*-positions something that has the same value or is equally important.

Here is a little thought process. Have you in the past few weeks recognized two positions in yourself, and thought: Do I in this one position think or do other things than in the other position? Can you indicate how you dealt with it (e.g., by having a conversation with yourself, or making other choices, or leaving it the way it is)?

If you have not immediately become aware of these differences, just think about it along the following lines: I as ... (in this situation), and I as ... (in another situation). Where do you detect the differences in these positions concerning your values, goals, and interests, and in your relations with other people? Can you write this down in some statements?

Background Information

If you take up a position regarding other people or yourself, then at a certain moment you will look at that position from a self-reflexive perspective. By doing so, you are assuming a "meta-position." This position is sometimes also described as a "helicopter view," because you are metaphorically looking down on yourself from high above and evaluating yourself. This only happens when you reflect on it afterwards. Let's take a look at this example. Teachers can critically evaluate their functioning as a teacher by distancing themselves from that role. They can do this only *after* having given a lecture. The best they can do *during* a lecture is concentrate completely on their teaching task and the interactions between themselves and their students. If they tried to critically observe themselves at the very moment when they are involved in the lecture, certain thoughts would distract them from the task. Only when looking back at their performance can they give themselves space and opportunity to critically evaluate their functioning as a teacher. At that moment, they look down on themselves, as if from a position above themselves, at how they are functioning, and they might ask themselves how they can improve themselves as teachers. Then they are in a meta-position.

Later at night, teachers still might think about a certain situation at school and what happened there. They realize that they occupy different positions. They are not just teachers, but also mentors, developers of a learning plan, and discussion partner for their students. But they think about this in a broader perspective. They also have relationships beyond their professional roles. They don't consider themselves as just a teacher, but also as a partner, and a parent. How do all these *I*-positions relate to each other? Can they be combined? How can an individual arrange their life so that everything can and will run smoothly? At that moment they rise, metaphorically speaking, upwards in a helicopter from which they can see more of their own *I*-positions. Only after having done this can they contemplate about the specific value of each position in their current and future life. By placing their positions in a broader context, and with an eye to the future, they can better decide in what direction they want to develop themselves.

To recapitulate: This example shows that you can find yourself positioned at three levels:

- as long you are in the middle of an activity, you find yourself *in* a position— no meta-position is involved here
- after you reflect on just that one position, you are in a meta-position—we call this a singular meta-position—you reflect on just *one* position, and you are going to reflect on that position from a distance

34 Part 1 Opposition

FIGURE 5.1 Take some time off to see the big picture and your direction in life
Source: Wikimedia Commons

- you can rise to a higher level by taking into consideration *several* positions—then you are in multiple meta-positions because you start to evaluate various and different positions.

You arrive at a "higher" meta-position because you look at and compare more specific positions, as if you are in a helicopter and rise up higher in the sky. You can then also notice the connections between the various *I*-positions, see where they "need help" to strengthen each other, but also where they are in conflict with each other and where there are possible frictions.

Consumption Behavior and Inner Contradiction

In her research on consumption behavior, Shalini Bahl (2012) found that from a meta-position you can take a critical look at your own consumption behavior. You want to have a beer because you want to relax; you want to use drugs because you want to enjoy your life; to eat a bag of chips to give yourself some comfort; to smoke a cigarette to have some peace of mind. So long as you are *in* such a position, it feels fine to do all these things, because then you act from spontaneous impulses that arise from that situation. But when we look at this behavior from the perspective of a meta-position, the situation might appear very different.

CONSUMER-CITIZEN: A POWERFUL COALITION

Canadian economist Sue McGregor (1999) was one of the first to propose that consumer and citizenship studies should be integrated. She recommended that people start to position themselves as "consumer-citizens" bringing together consumer interests and citizen ethics. This implies that people begin to see themselves as being engaged in a life-long socialization process, in which they balance the interest of others (e.g., people in developing countries and future generations), and also the environment, against self-interest in the marketplace. Citizens who act as responsible consumers think ahead and temper their desires through social awareness, and are prepared to sacrifice personal pleasure to communal well-being. Their actions in the marketplace are construed as impacting citizenship, and vice versa. In her view, the ultimate educational objective of citizenship education is an increased rate and higher quality of social participation. Democratic citizens deliberate with other citizens about the nature of the common collective good and how to achieve it. They do so via debate, deliberation, agenda-setting, making public judgments, performing community services, supporting and working for public interest groups and political parties. The result should be an education that prepares citizens, via their individual and collective actions, to pursue the common good rather than just advancing their private, individual self-interest.

The coalition of the consumer and citizen positions has enormous potential to influence and change consumption patterns on the macro-level. The internet, in particular, offers excellent opportunities for consumers to rapidly communicate with each other and organize themselves collectively in order to influence and correct consumption patterns that are undesirable from a citizen perspective. As marketing specialists, Behrang Rezabakhsh and colleagues (2006) have noticed that the internet enables consumers to overcome lack of information that characterizes traditional consumer markets, and thus obtain high levels of market transparency. Also, they can easily band together against companies and impose sanctions by terminating business or consumption relationships, and they have an effective communication channel available for sharing and spreading negative consumption experiences. The internet enables them to take a more active role in influencing products and prices according to the preferences they have as responsible citizens in a global society.

This way, you might come to realize that there can be certain behavior patterns that are less healthy when viewed from a long-term perspective. The meta-position offers a broader view of the positions you occupy in your life, and from that perspective you realize that it isn't very wise to smoke a cigarette or to drink

FIGURE 5.2 The "power" of consumer-citizens
Source: Wikimedia Commons

a lot of alcohol. What this means is that the feelings you have at a lower level (e. g., I as a hedonist, I as a social human being, I as someone who seeks comfort) can be completely different from the feelings you have when you are in a meta-position. From the perspective of this position, you are saying: "I like this but I realize that it is actually not good for me." At that moment an inner contradiction arises that facilitates an evaluation of your behavior from a wider perspective in order to correct it, if necessary. The meta-position often gives you different information from the specific situation-related *I*-position. To assume a meta-position means that you can guide your behavior in accordance with the goals you have for the future.

Characteristics of a Meta-position

To understand the concept of a meta-position, we now summarize its most important characteristics.

- It facilitates taking a *distance* from your immediate and impulsive behavior so that you can evaluate it from an external viewpoint. Think about the example of teachers who reflect critically on how they teach their classes.
- The meta-position offers *insight* that allows you to inter-connect and evaluate various behavioral processes. It enables you to evaluate different positions (*I*-positions) in relation to one another. You are not looking just at a specific behavioral act, but at the entire configuration of behaviors and positions,

where they originate from, and what their consequences are. Think about the example of an unhealthy consumptive behavior that in due course has evolved into a habit.

- You develop an insight into the *history* of an *I*-position. Think about someone you know with an addiction. How did they develop the addiction, what happened before that? Did it originate from a feeling of loneliness, or did it start with a new circle of friends? Meta-positions can help you understand how one position can overflow into another one. That can occur with addictive behavior—but also with every recurring behavioral process.
- A meta-position can also function as a point of direction for the *future*. From this particular position you might be able to make plans for the future by reflecting on several *I*-positions. By considering how your different *I*-positions relate to one another, and by recognizing tensions and conflicts between them, you might be able to make better judgments and decisions. Moreover, a meta-position can break through habits and embedded behavioral patterns. This can lead to various decisions, such as breaking off certain contacts that you no longer view as important, or changing your consumer behavior, your travel style, or your study habits. And from that position you can also develop new initiatives for the future (see the example above where we discussed the position of a consumer versus the position as a citizen).

A meta-position, especially the multiple variant of it, offers a helicopter view from which you can observe multiple *I*-positions. You can analyze the differences and similarities between them and gain insights into their origins. At the same time, you can notice the various implications for your future. That way you can act, evaluate, and draw consequences based on the values and goals you have derived from those *I*-positions.

Distancing Yourself versus Impulsive Responses

Assuming a meta-position seems to be good for controlling our emotions. This is evident in researchers' findings that keeping a distance from our intense emotions has a favorable effect on our mental health (Kross, Ayduk & Mischel, 2005). If people stick to their negative emotions (e.g., anger or anxiety) about things that happened in the past, they often typically show a closed or rigid position. They are inclined to look around from just that one dominant position and do not change their perspectives. From their original position, they proceed very selectively and seem to remember only negatively colored events that confirm their original negative experience. These people re-experience such events as if they had happened only recently, and are not able to look at those experiences from a more distanced and evaluative view. As long as they can't perceive those experiences from a more distanced view, their emotions stay intense and cannot be altered. Re-processing of emotions is possible only if we can distance ourselves from our initial or primary emotion. You then look at your emotional responses from the outside, as if they occurred in someone else. Such a distancing position makes it possible for the level of intensity to decrease so that we can assume other perspectives without the necessity of giving up the memory of the negative event.

Elaborating on this insight, Kross and colleagues (2005) came up with the idea of asking subjects in their experiments to remember an event in which they felt overwhelmed by anger and hostility. Then they invited the subjects to re-imagine this experience in a very vivid way or, alternatively, to take a step back from it. To *re-invoke* the experience, they gave the subjects the following instructions: Go back to the time and place where you experienced this emotion and try to re-imagine it as intensely as possible, as if it is happening to you here and now. *Distance* became evoked by telling the subjects: Just take some steps back from your experience and look at it as if you are watching a play in a theater.

THE PARADOX OF SOLOMON

To gain insight into the process of taking distance, we think the paradox of Solomon is extremely valuable. Solomon, leader of the Jewish people, was known for his wisdom and thoughtful judgment. It is less well-known that he made a mess of his own personal life. He made bad decisions and let himself be directed by uncontrolled emotions. He loved money, bragged about his financial wealth, and had, spread over the years, a harem of 700 wives and 300 concubines. He also neglected to give his son a good education.

Here is a paradox: Solomon was a very wise man when he had to give advice to other people, but he couldn't apply that wisdom to matters in his own life. Inspired by this paradox, researchers invited people between the ages of 20 and 40 to imagine that they were betrayed by a friend (Grossman & Kross, 2014). Then they asked the subjects how they would react in a situation like that. As in the Solomon paradox, they found that the subjects in their experiments could not consider their limited knowledge about the event very well, could not assume a different perspective, and were not willing to look for a compromise. However, they showed more appropriate behavior when they were asked to give advice to a person who was betrayed by a friend. The fascinating aspect about this research is that afterwards the researchers asked the subjects to distance themselves from their own emotions. When that happened, their advice to themselves had the same quality as the advice given to another person. Taking distance from yourself subdues the emotion, without fully pushing it (the emotion) away, and due to the spectator position it promotes a more informed judgment.

The researchers also asked the subjects to look at their emotional experience through a "what-question": What were your emotions and what happened to you? And from a "why-question": What was the reason you got so angry; What made your anger so intense? It then appeared that the subjects who had assumed a distancing position, and at the same time asked themselves the why-question, were less bothered by the emotion than the subjects who had focused themselves on the emotion, and asked themselves just about the what-question. It appears that assuming a meta-position triggers a person to take a distance from their own emotion, and concentrate on the why-question of this emotion.

Summarizing

- A meta-position facilitates a helicopter view. With the singular variant, we reflect only about *one* I-position. With multiple variants, we can consider a wider range of positions and evaluate them in their relation to each other and their history.
- A meta-position has four important characteristics:

  you distance yourself from specific positions;
  you obtain insight into the connections between positions;
  the history of those positions becomes clear; and
  it offers a perspective on the future so that habits can be stopped.

- Self-distance leads to regulation of emotions.
- Self-distance promotes wise decisions.
- Self-distance promotes inner contradiction: there is a counterbalance regarding more dominant positions that would otherwise completely dominate your behavior repertoire.

Critical questions

In the text we assumed a rather important presupposition: We can make better decisions about our life and our behavior if we can assume a meta-position. We can even become wiser from it. The reason is that we can deal with our emotions better when taking a meta-position.

- But, we can ask, is that really the case? Does it help you when you regularly look at yourself from a meta-position? Also, does the text establish sufficient evidence for that supposition, and how is it substantiated? Is this an example of self-critical thinking?

40 Part 1 Opposition

- Can you detect in the text more presuppositions that make you doubt it? Can you formulate those in a question and discuss them with other people?

Exercise

Choose an *I*-position for yourself: for example, I as a student, or I as a son/daughter. Describe that *I*-position from the perspective of another person who knows you very well in that position (e.g., a fellow student, or a sibling). This (hypothetical) other person takes the position of the third person and speaks about you as "he" or "she," and only uses your first name to provide a narrative about you. For this exercise it is important that you hold on to this assignment:

[NAME] is a fellow student of mine. He or she is a student at our school.

Then zoom in on a painful situation that he or she (actually you!) has recently experienced: A bad evaluation of an internship, or a situation at school, or a conflict, or something else that is bothering you. What happened emotionally? How did that happen, and why did it happen? What kind of advice would you give? [This can be an uncomfortable exercise.]

It all depends on whether you have the courage to look at yourself through the eyes of another person. And you have to maintain this position in a consistent way, at least for a while. Then you might discover aspects of yourself that you didn't notice before, when you were looking and thinking solely from the perspective of your own individual self.

Reflecting

- Are you ready, at this point, to assume a meta-position? That meta-position starts by reflecting on your different *I*-positions.
- And can you form a picture of the similarities and differences between those *I*-positions by looking at the values that are important to you, that originated from those *I*-positions? What happens when you think about certain goals you are trying to reach, when you examine the emotions you are experiencing, and look at the pattern in those positions?
- Can you now go back to what you have said in "From Your Own Experience" at the start of this chapter? Do you want to add or change something? Have you learned anything in this chapter that has an impact on your initial description? If so, what? Do you think you want to make some changes to those positions, or change them completely? Do you think you can succeed in this endeavor?

6

TOLERANCE OF UNCERTAINTY

Helpful or Unhelpful?

Generally, uncertainty is experienced as unpleasant. Yet it is not just a negative experience. In some senses, it might be helpful to becoming citizens in this world. How can we use "uncertainty" in a productive way, and how can it help us in our contact with others and ourselves?

From Your Own Experience

What issues and situations are you uncertain about? The future, yourself, other people, spread of virus, climate change? Do you find it very unpleasant to experience uncertainty? Or can uncertainty also be pleasant? Can you indicate when and where you find uncertainty pleasant or unpleasant? Can uncertainty be good for something, or not good at all? Write your thoughts down in a few sentences.

Background Information

In general, we experience uncertainty as a negative feeling. There are many situations in which we feel uncertain and strongly prefer certainty over uncertainty. For example, it is rather annoying when you do not know where you have stored a certain item, and you might even doubt yourself and tell yourself that you know for sure that you had put it away in a certain place, but you don't know where. Or when your father or mother has not come home at a certain time—that is a very unpleasant uncertainty. Where are they? Has anything bad happened to them? We get nervous from uncertainty, and we seem not to cope with it very well. Just pay attention to the word itself. "Uncertainty" is a "un" word, it has a negative connotation, just like unpleasant, unregulated, unfit, unfriendly, or unbearable, all words that signify something unpleasant.

42 Part 1 Opposition

However, this is not the entire story. Uncertainty can also be experienced as a positive feeling. We experience this when we watch an exciting movie, and the climax is revealed much later. Or we want to explore a landscape that is new to us, because the unknown aspect of it is exactly what attracts us. Or we watch a sports game, and it's uncertain who will win or lose. Not knowing the result in these situations is exactly what is exciting to us. There is a gulf between the completely known, which can be experienced as "boring," and the completely unknown, that can be experienced as "frightening." The area in between those extremes is loaded with a tension that can feel unpleasant or exciting.

Because this book deals with inner democracy, it is important that we pay attention to the broader societal structure in which we participate as members of society. In our society, we are confronted with developments that can contribute to our feeling of uncertainty. Consider robot technology. On one hand, this advanced technology can accomplish a lot of unpleasant tasks that human beings don't or can't do; but on the other hand, this technology might take over human jobs we consider as important in society at large. This is a conflict. Or consider globalization, that stimulates trade across borders but also results in the moving of jobs to different countries, often with much lower wages. Or consider the influx of social media, that offers new possibilities of keeping in contact with other people around the world but can also lead to new addictions. A temporary shut-down to stop the spread of coronavirus is unpleasant but it also reduces air-pollution. These developments are intriguing, and it is unclear how these many aspects are interwoven in our day-to-day life. These are just some examples of developments for which no immediate resolution is available and over which people tend to disagree. But the examples also indicate that the uncertainty linked to these developments can generate in us both positive and negative feelings. Some people experience these developments as unfavorable and consider them as threatening, while other people find them desirable and view them as new challenges for the future.

Uncertainty: How do we Deal with it?

An important question is: How do we react to uncertainty? We cannot give an unambiguous answer to this question because people differ enormously in how they deal with uncertainty.

In the research that we describe in the box below, employees in a certain company chose entirely different ways of responding to a situation that can be characterized as uncertain. These responses are also dependent on the I-positions they have at their disposal in their behavioral repertoires. One person can react from a fatalistic point of view ("It's my destiny to always run out of luck"), or from a victim-position ("Why is this always happening to me? I'm always the fall guy"), and get depressed.

RESPONSES TO UNCERTAINTY ARE HIGHLY DIFFERENT

People respond very differently to situations of uncertainty. In an extensive study, Dex and colleagues (2000) researched how people reacted to big changes in their work situation. They studied 28,000 employees from British companies who, during the years 1980–1990, were confronted with enormous uncertainty as a consequence of new legislation, increasing competition, and changes in technology. The researchers found that these complex changes were experienced by the employees as problematic. But they also noticed that some employees reacted very differently to the changes. Some people just kept working at the same company and didn't undertake anything else, while others went looking for another job. Some individuals continued as part-timers and went looking for second jobs to increase their income. And there were also people who started informal networks to support each other, and some people tried to find as much information as possible about alternative possibilities for their future. It was striking to see that many employees started to capitalize on the new situation in a timely and constructive way.

Other people react in a more assertive way. They see the new situation as a challenge ("I'm going to explore new possibilities"), or feel themselves supported by family members ("My family supports me"), or use their network ("I'm going to contact some colleagues who might be able to help me").

In terms of the theory presented in this book, we can view an uncertain situation as a dynamic process of positioning and counter-positioning, as described in Chapter 1. Those who confront a threatening situation can see themselves as victims ("It always happens to me"), and react in a way that only further confirms that initial position ("It's always me who is threatened with dismissal"). However, those who react to a threat of dismissal with expressions like "I as explorative" or "I feel supported by my network" react with a counter-position from a perspective that offers alternative possibilities (think about the three-step model described in Chapter 4), and then there is a possibility that a new road can be travelled. This is the process of re-positioning we described earlier with the term "flexibility." People can be motivated to make use of this flexibility only if their position-repertoire is sufficiently broad and varied to invoke positions that allow them to go in another direction.

Citizen and Consumer: Two Worlds

Let's take this argument one step further, beyond just the question of how to respond to situations of uncertainty. We propose that allowing some degree of uncertainty in some situations might be advisable. We can illustrate this by

44 Part 1 Opposition

looking at the relation between two important *I*-positions: I as a consumer, and I as a citizen.

We all buy goods and services from our position as a consumer. As long as we operate as a consumer, we can buy all we want provided that we have sufficient financial means. Shops and commercial organizations use all means to help us as much as possible in our consumer behavior. But when we think about the effect of consumption on the environment, our ecological footprint, such as the consequences of air traffic for our climate, then we assume the *I*-position of me as citizen. If we take into consideration the ecological consequences of our consumer behavior for our planet, we might even find ourselves in the position of "I as citizen of the world."

The two positions, I as consumer and I as citizen, each carry their own responsibilities. As a consumer, I want to take good care of myself and the people who I feel close to. Through my consumer behavior, I also contribute to the economy on a wider scale. As a citizen, I share responsibility for society at large and also for the environment. Our interests, values, objectives—in short, our responsibilities in these two *I*-positions—can lead us in two different directions and so we end up in a situation of uncertainty.

From the theory of inner democracy, we learned that it is advisable not just to act from *one* *I*-position, but, confronted with various choices, always to take into consideration the objectives, values, and responsibilities from a broader variety of *I*-positions. This can result in a feeling of uncertainty because a specific choice is no longer limited to just one *I*-position. You swerve for a short period between two positions. One position is confronted by the other position. Only then are you going to make a choice. Only then is there a chance that you can make a choice not just from your needs as a consumer, but also from your preferences as a responsible citizen. We are not suggesting that all your behavior should result from one or the other position. What we propose is that you conduct an inner dialogue from both those positions and then come to a decision. Suppose you are used to eating hamburgers, but the restaurant also offers tasty vege-burgers. What do you choose? Or, some people are used to flying for vacation four times a year, but they could consider going twice a year, each time for a longer duration. What should they do?[1]

And thus the expression "I as a citizen" functions as a position that is sometimes in conflict with "I as a consumer," and this leads to inner contradictions that can give our decisions a wider base than if we blindly follow only one of our *I*-positions.

The Ethical Purchasing Gap

Although consumers are increasingly interested in making ethical purchasing decisions as responsible citizens, significant differences exist between consumers' ethical intentions and their actual purchasing behavior. This discrepancy between

FIGURE 6.1 Shall we survive?
Source: Unsplash

what we prefer and what we actually do has been coined by Cowe & Williams (2000) as the "ethical purchasing gap." In a large-scale study in the UK, these investigators found that more than one third of consumers described themselves as "ethical purchasers," yet on the level of actual consumer behavior it appeared that ethically accredited products counted for only 3 percent of the purchases. Motivated by this finding, Bray, Johns & Kilburn (2011) wondered about the motives behind this gap. They organized three focus group discussions, each consisting of six consumers, and found a variety of motives that impeded ethical purchase behavior. Some of them are summarized here.

Price sensitivity

Participants in the focus groups often mentioned price, indicating that financial considerations were more important to them than ethical values, particularly with reference to food and other frequently purchased items. As one participant remarked: "I don't … consider ethical products in a supermarket because it's a bill you pay weekly and you want it to be as small as possible."

Brand allegiance

Aside from the price, group members admitted that their allegiance to certain brands prevented them from moving towards an overtly ethical option. Typical endorsements of brand loyalty were: "I'm a Heinz person"; "Got to have your Weetabix in the morning." Such brand attachments were accepted by the

46 Part 1 Opposition

participants in the focus groups although they did not necessarily consider them as ethically correct.

Quality perception

Some participants made it clear that they perceived products branded "Fair Trade" as poorer in quality. But others believed that happy chicken tasted nicer (better), with the result that their search for quality drove them to ethical consumption. In general, the perceived quality of ethical goods was clearly an influencing factor in the decision-making process of some participants in this research.

Cynicism

Many participants had the feeling that ethical claims were just another marketing ploy, seducing consumers to pay higher prices by taking advantage of their goodwill. They believed that most of the extra premium that was paid did not reach the end beneficiary, and that a large part of it was intercepted by corporate or governmental organizations. For some participants, this was a key factor in their decision to disregard ethical products. As one participant remarked: "It's purely for company profit. I think it begins and ends there."

The ethical purchasing gap may be a challenge, and even a threat, to a balanced relationship between our position as consumer who is concerned about getting the best product for the best price, and as a citizen who is engaged in the welfare of the world community. As the findings of Bray and colleagues (2011) suggest, to play a proper role in the decision process as consumers in a world confronted with depletion of resources and climate change, we have to take into account factors that impede the citizen position. However, if we acknowledge both positions, I as consumer and I as citizen, in our decision processes, we have to face a degree of uncertainty because we can no longer act purely on the basis of just one position.

Strategies for Dealing with Uncertainty

How do people deal with situations that can be characterized as highly uncertain, and how do they strategize their position-repertoire? Hermans & Hermans-Konopka (2010) distinguish four different strategies for reducing a high level of uncertainty.

1. Uncertainty can be managed by considerably *reducing the number and variety of I-positions*. We become aware of this reaction when we see people in a stressful situation decide to lead a simpler life. They find themselves in a situation that evokes a cacophony of voices in themselves, triggering confusion and feelings of being overwhelmed. They no longer feel at ease in

certain situations, and can only escape from those situations by avoiding certain contacts as much as possible. They no longer go to gatherings, festivities, or other group activities. They no longer participate on platforms such as Facebook, or wish to be involved in WhatsApp groups. Maybe they even decide to go on living somewhere else, in a quieter environment, driven by a desire for a calmer and simpler life.

2. Uncertainty can also be reduced by *giving a leading role to just one I-position* which then comes to dominate the entire repertoire of positions. When people need to find their way in an unclear situation and do not know what road to take, it is easier to hand over responsibility to an authority figure, a guru, a strongman, or "godfather" and thereby make the situation more transparent. These people then find themselves in a position of docility in which they neglect their own position as an active and responsible citizen by saying: "Just let someone else make the decision." We see this, for instance, in people who follow the leader of an utopian movement or a guru who delivers a certain message in the form of a simplistic doctrine.

3. One way to reduce the level of uncertainty is *hardening the boundaries between "us" and "them."* Rigid boundaries are set up between the "ingroup" (the group to which you belong) and the "outgroup" (the group to which you do not belong, or do not want to belong). In doing so, we assign a higher status to the members of the ingroup than to the members of the outgroup. We notice this in expressions such as "we're not like them," "we enjoy more privileges than they do," or "they're inferior to us." This reaction has left a trail throughout history. It has happened, and it is still happening, that entire groups of a population exclude each other and exhibit discriminatory behavior. We see this in the history of African Americans in the USA and of Jews in Europe, and also in prejudices about women, and in animosity toward transgender people. Discriminatory behavior can be found at all times, and we can offer many examples. Currently we are seeing, even in democratic countries, signs of this kind of discriminatory behavior, for example from people who, out of fear of the "Islamification" of Europe, are willing to stereotype various groups in a population without any differentiation. Not wanting to differentiate among members of an outgroup is characteristic of the hardening of boundaries between "us" and "them." This hardening of positions can obstruct a flexible change in the position-repertoire.

4. An alternative for dealing with uncertainty, one that contributes to inner democracy, is developing *tolerance for uncertainty*, instead of avoiding it. As we mentioned earlier, an ambiguous situation often evokes an unpleasant feeling, and we would rather do without it. However, it is important that we acknowledge the existence and the constructive aspects of uncertainty. The complex character of the world around us is a given fact and it is better to face this than to deny it. Moreover, we could try to make positive use of

48 Part 1 Opposition

feelings of uncertainty in particular situations. We can accomplish this when we use our ability to suspend judgment (see Chapter 3). When we experience uncertainty as an unpleasant emotion, then we might be inclined to immediately make a judgment about a certain group of people or a specific situation. But the disadvantage here is that we no longer allow alternative viewpoints, and a flexible change in perspective is no longer possible. If we are willing to suspend our judgment and allow ourselves to take up a meta-position, preferably multiple meta-positions (see Chapter 5), then this is only possible when we accept a certain degree of uncertainty. We have seen that some *I*-positions can differ from, or even be contradictory to, each other. Assuming a meta-position inevitably invokes a feeling of uncertainty. At the same time, this so-called helicopter view broadens our perspective and then we become aware of alternative points of view. These viewpoints will remain invisible as long as we make use of one of the strategies we have discussed above for reducing uncertainty: Reducing the number of available *I*-positions, transferring our responsibilities to an authority figure, or permanently sharpening the boundaries of our *I*-positions and of the group to which we belong. In that context we referred to the three-step model (see Chapter 4). According to this model, we allow our initial position to be influenced by another position, either coming from someone else or as a result of our inner dialogue, and we then revise or change our original point of view. At this moment, uncertainty comes into play. After all, if the viewpoint of someone else is different from mine, then to a certain extent I have to try to allow for a feeling of uncertainty in acknowledging that my original viewpoint is not the only correct one. And this leads to having an inner dialogue with myself that can broaden my points of view and result in new ones.

We can easily recognize these four responses to the feeling of uncertainty in our daily lives, and all four can occur within the same individual at different moments. Sometimes we want to withdraw into our own "niche" when everything seems to have become too overwhelming (strategy 1). There can come a moment when we feel the urge to say to someone who always seems to know everything better: "I will leave it to you, you can handle it" (strategy 2). And at other moments we resist the invading distraction or complicated information that impacts our daily lives and we distance ourselves, for a little while, from the outside world (strategy 3). But sometimes we take a step back and acknowledge "I feel uncertain about this" and then, in a conversation with a friend or yourself, you stand open to a new idea that can help you with taking the next step (strategy 4).

Summarizing

- People react rather differently to situations of uncertainty. Their responses are co-determined by the *I*-positions in their repertoire.

- Uncertainty can be useful in situations where we are confronted with different alternatives. As an example, we discussed the relation between I as a consumer and I as a citizen.
- Four different strategies were discussed to cope with uncertainty: (1) reducing the number of available *I*-positions; (2) transferring responsibility to certain authorities; (3) closing off the boundaries between the ingroup you belong to and members of outgroups; and preferably (4) allowing uncertainty and making fruitful use of it.
- Allowing uncertainty is involved in almost all the topics we have discussed previously: alternative viewpoints (Can you see another way of looking at a particular problem?); suspension of judgment (Can you postpone your immediate reaction?); flexible changing of perspective (Can you change or adapt your initial point of view?); assuming a multiple meta-position (Can you take a helicopter view on your different *I*-positions?). Reflection on those possibilities helps us to acquire new viewpoints and discover new behavioral responses.

FIGURE 6.2 Uncertainty requires us to explore different roads
Source: Unsplash

50 Part 1 Opposition

Critical Questions

In this chapter we described the feeling of uncertainty as a mainly positive force. Contradiction often produces uncertainty. We wanted to show that you need to have tolerance for uncertainty in order to deal with contradictions.

- Do you think we have demonstrated in a convincing way that it is valuable to allow for uncertainty? What are your arguments for and against?
- Do you have any questions about certain parts of the text? What are your questions, and can you discuss them with others?

Exercise

This is an exercise for two people who play two different "roles." Each person will also take the alternative role.

Write down an opinion in which you firmly believe and about which you have strong feelings. Formulate this opinion in a sentence with the following structure: "I feel certain that …" Write underneath a few points about why you believe in this point of view so strongly. Then, for each of the points you have mentioned, describe whether you hold a flexible or a more closed-off position regarding each point.

When you (person A) have finished this write-up, hand over your sheet of paper to another student (person B) in your group. B then prepares him or herself for a conversation with you in which they give conflicting or contradicting remarks. B tries to put him or herself in the position of you, A, who wrote the opinion. Which *I*-position might underlie that conviction? What other *I*-positions of A can function as a counter-position? B then starts a conversation with A in which B tries very hard to persuade A to strongly doubt their opinion. Try to focus especially on the points that A earmarked as closed-off positions. Then reverse the roles. And then, after this role-play, you will both have a conversation with each other.

- Start a conversation with each other. Are you successful in persuading the other person to doubt their own original position?
- How does their uncertainty manifest itself? How serious is this feeling of uncertainty? Can you make a productive use of the resulting uncertainty?

Reflecting

- Contradictions can occur in your inner self when you choose or create a counter-position versus a dominant *I*-position. And then a dialogue ensues between those positions.

- Can you entertain an inner conversational dialogue? Have you ever used this in a particular situation? How did you feel about it? What sometimes makes it difficult to have an inner conversation?
- If you have not been engaged in a conflicting conversation within yourself recently: what prevented you from doing so? What would facilitate this conversation within your inner self?
- At the start of this chapter you wrote in "From Your Own Experience" when and where, in certain situations, you notice uncertainty as pleasant or unpleasant, and if uncertainty can be good in certain circumstances. Have you noticed any changes? If so, can you describe these?

Note

1. For the question of how to be a responsible tourist, see Sampson (2020).

7

EMOTION AND REASON

Can They Hold Hands?

In our thought processes, we usually expect to start out with our reasoning capacities. We always see it formulated this way, but quite often the opposite is happening. Our emotions play a much larger role in our inner experiential life than we expect. In this chapter we explore the ways you can deal with possible conflicts between emotion and reason.

From Your Own Experience

Let's return to the opinion you wrote down in the exercise at the end of Chapter 6. What made you so sure of this opinion? Do you have reasons for it, or did feelings and emotions play a role too? And can you describe what happened to you during the conversation? Did you use just your reasoning capacities? Or did emotions also come into play? Which emotions played a role? Think about a discussion you might have had recently with another person, a discussion in which you expressed a firm and strong belief about a certain subject.

Background Information

We have two important capacities to deal with the world and ourselves: our reason and our emotions. Reason enables us to think in a logical way, to analyze things, and to compare them to each other and come to conclusions. It helps us to explore the origins of phenomena and provide rational explanations for them. We need our reasoning to investigate complex and problematic situations and consider pro's and con's on our way to finding solutions.

An emotion is an affective state associated with a degree of pleasure or displeasure, such as an experience of happiness, anxiety, or sorrow. This state can be invoked by a specific situation and can arise spontaneously. Emotions can be accompanied by bodily reactions, facial expressions, or impulsive behavioral acts. Events we consider as threatening or harmful can lead to feelings of fear, anxiety, or anger. These unpleasant emotions motivate us to withdraw, to fight-or-flight, or to look for safety. Events we associate with a reward invoke positive feelings of joy, safety, or a pleasant surprise. Instead of withdrawing or defending ourselves, we initiate approaching behavior and search for contact (e.g., approaching an attractive person, or making up with somebody after a fight).

There are moments when reason and emotion are in nice harmony with each other. They are then well coordinated and both influence our behavior. For example, if I decide to stop heavy physical training, my reasoning voice says "I have many reasons to stop," and my emotion says "I don't like this any more." This decision is then based on an agreement between my reason and my emotion.

However, it can also happen that reason and emotion are in conflict with each other and drive us to contrary behavioral responses. Suppose you get a very disturbing message via email or WhatsApp that makes you rather upset. Your immediate impulsive reaction is to write an angry response that shows clearly how you feel about it. But after a little while, you stop and ask yourself: What do I want to accomplish with this, and is it wise to react in such an angry way? Then a process of balancing can start in which your reasoning processes also play a role. You then realize that the message you wanted to send might give you immediate relief, but it might also run the risk that contact with the other person gets disrupted, and this is something you want to prevent. In this case emotion and reason are in conflict with each other. However, after contemplating several alternative responses, you might be able to formulate a less emotionally laden answer that is also in agreement with your reasoning.

In short, there are situations in which emotion and reason easily complement each other. But they can also clash with each other. When this happens, a dialogue arises in which the original position (your emotional response) provokes a response in the form of a counter-positioning (your reasoning). At the end of this dialogue, a decision can be reached that feels "better" because both "parties" are in agreement with each other. This process can be described as a reason–emotion dialogue.

The Relation between Reason and Emotion

The relation between reason and emotion has been the subject of numerous treatises in philosophy from Plato to Descartes. Until well into the 20th century, many scientists thought that emotions are necessarily in conflict with reason, and therefore need to be controlled. The presumption was that the "correct" insight was given by reasoning alone, and that emotion stands in the way of reason and interferes with "well-thought" solutions to problems. You cannot trust emotions

54 Part 1 Opposition

because they render human beings as "unreasonable" and it is only reason that stands "above" emotion, that can lead to "correct" behavior.

However, this view that advocates "reason above emotion" has been challenged by brain scientists. One of the most important critiques of this view (Damasio, 1994) was based on neurological research that yielded (advocated) a theory that considered emotions as appropriate reactions in a variety of situations. It is a well-known phenomenon that fear increases our heartbeat when we see a dangerous animal and we know immediately that we have to protect ourselves. Or, we feel sad and cry when we are touched by someone or something and feel motivated to give solace to a certain person or feel compassion about what is happening in the world. According to this theory, emotional-physical processes are also very important for making decisions. If people were motivated only by their reasoning capacities, it would be difficult to make decisions because they would be reasoning endlessly before coming to a conclusion. In some cases it would be better to listen to your emotions because that would give you information about your preferences. Our emotions can help us in making easier and faster decisions. Emotion and reason work together in this respect. Our reasoning is not something that stands above emotion, but stands next to it; emotion and reason embrace each other, they are partners as in an Argentine Tango.

The Value of "Negative" Emotions

It is a well-known misunderstanding to conceive positive emotions as only desirable and negative emotions as only undesirable. On the contrary, so-called "negative" emotions can sometimes be very valuable. Suppose you have had a conversation with someone and afterwards you have an unpleasant feeling, or perhaps a feeling of "emptiness", but you can't really formulate what is bothering you. Only afterward, you realize that the person with whom you had this conversation was saying all kinds of interesting things, but when you yourself expressed something, the discussion transferred immediately back to your conversation partner and focused on their viewpoints. You realize that this conversation looks more like a monolog than a dialogue, and you now understand how this feeling of emptiness arose. Thanks to this original inexplicable feeling, you have more insight into what you had missed in the conversation. Your reason goes in the the "right direction" after you listen to your emotion. The fact that a feeling can be experienced as negative doesn't mean that it is not useful. Where would we be if we did not experience any feelings of guilt? After all, those feelings can put you in a direction to undertake something to make set things right. The same explanation applies to feelings of confusion. These experiences aren't necessarily useless because they can motivate you to re-order your thoughts. Confusion often leads to exploring and finding new ways to solve a problem. Like uncertainty, confusion often opens the path to breaking with rigid thoughts or behavioral patterns, and can make you even more creative.

Being angry or upset also has desirable side effects, as it can help you to defend yourself in situations where your own self-interest is at stake. When it becomes clear that somebody has misled you on purpose, expressing your anger may be helpful to make it perfectly clear that this behavior is unacceptable.

A Higher and Lower Circuit in Our Brain

To understand the relation between reason and emotion, it is important to realize that we are not always conscious of our emotions, and that they are not accessible at every given moment to our reason. Developments in the neurosciences are helpful to understand why emotions are only partly under the control of our reason. One scientist who has contributed significantly to this insight is LeDoux (2002), who showed that there are two circuits in our brain that transmit emotions: a higher and a lower circuit. The lower circuit comes into action when a stimulus arrives at the amygdala, the center of emotion, that then gives a signal leading to a fast physical reaction (e.g., flight-or-fight). Simultaneously, a circuit opens up between the amygdala and the pre-frontal cortex, the center of our higher brain functions, where we become conscious of our emotions. At that level, we arrive at self-reflection and self-control. However, the lower circuit transmits its signal twice as fast as the higher circuit. That is why the self-conscious brain cannot stop the emotional reaction in a timely way. And this happens when we shrink back if suddenly we see an unclear figure appearing in the darkness, or when we snarl at somebody before we realize that we should maybe act differently. This means that "I as a reasonable person" is not immediately

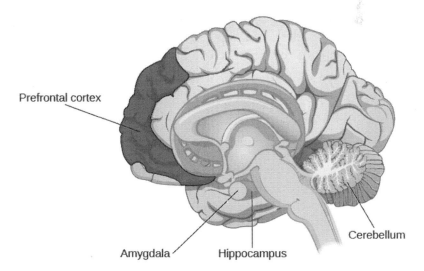

FIGURE 7.1 Location of the prefrontal cortex and amygdala
Courtesy: Lumen Learning

56 Part 1 Opposition

available to function as an effective counter-position in relation to the faster "I-as-emotional" position. That explains why we often offer apologies for our emotional behavior and responses over which we have no control.

Paying Attention Enlarges Our Sensitivity

The fact that the lower circuit is faster than the higher one doesn't mean that it is impossible to improve our sensitivity to our emotions. The key concept here is *attention*. By paying attention we can delve more deeply into our more-or-less unconscious emotions, recognize them earlier, and thereby bring them under control. Brain scientists Dehaene & Naccache (2001) observed that we can increase our sensitivity to stimuli by "attentional amplification" (this means literally strengthening via attention). They show that via "attention-giving" we can activate top-down circuits through which less conscious stimuli of our perception can penetrate. This means that stimuli of which we are normally not aware can be perceived by us if we pay sufficient attention to them.

By focusing our attention, not only perceptual stimuli can be observed sooner, but emotional stimuli as well. This line of thought is central in the work of Edwards & Jacobs (2003) who, building on the oeuvre of Carl Jung, argue that a dialogue is possible between the conscious and unconscious layers in ourselves by first invoking unconscious emotions. They asked subjects in their research to project themselves in different situations, via painting or drawing, dancing, or making sculptures. Only afterwards can participants look at their own results in a conscious way and then formulate some coherent thoughts about it. In this dialogue between the unconscious and the conscious level, it is essential to pay attention to oneself via the artistic products, unconscious emotions, and desires that consequently are subjected to self-reflection.[1]

Contradiction between Emotional Intolerance and Reason

When we talk about promoting inner democracy, it is important that we pay attention to the emotions that might arise when we meet groups of people we dislike. The question we are confronted with here is: To what extent are we tolerant or intolerant of population groups that differ strongly from us, especially when those groups evoke ambivalent emotions in us? How do those emotions relate to our reasoning?

In their revealing article "Democratization and political tolerance in seventeen countries" (2003), political scientists Peffley and Rohrschneider point to the rise of democracies in the world since World War II, such as in Spain, Portugal, Italy, the Balkan countries, and in Africa, South America, and the Middle East.[2] At the same time, support for democratic governmental institutions is very high. Citizens strongly favor democratic principles such as freedom of speech, freedom to hold elections, and the right to demonstrate. A growing number of people in the world advocate the protection of their rights by democratic institutions (i.e., rule of law, adherence to institutions, and parliamentary representation).

In their challenging research project, Peffley and colleagues studied the levels of political tolerance in seventeen democratic countries that claim political tolerance. In this study, political tolerance was defined as "the willingness to allow expression of ideas and interests that you disagree with" (2003, p. 243). First, the respondents were asked to select from a list of seven groups the one they disliked most: immigrants, Jews, capitalists, homosexuals, Stalinists, criminals, and neo-Nazis (Figure 7.2). Then the respondents were asked: "Do you think that members of the groups you just have chosen, should be allowed (a) to hold public office and (b) to openly demonstrate"? The results were astonishing because they conflicted sharply with the overall principle of the principle of equality of democracy. Of the seventeen countries, the least amount of tolerance of the first question was found in Bosnia and Herzegovina. Just 1.4 percent of the respondents answered that they would give people of a group that they said they disliked the right to hold a public office. The highest percentage was found in the USA, where 14.4 percent agreed to give this right to a group they disliked. Even in established democracies such as in the Scandinavian countries, the percentages were very low.

Here we encounter a rather striking inconsistency. Respondents apparently think it is natural to appear as democratic, while on the other hand they behave undemocratically by saying they do not want to grant citizen rights to members of a group they dislike. If they approve of democracy as a desirable form of government, they seem not to be aware of the presence of another voice in

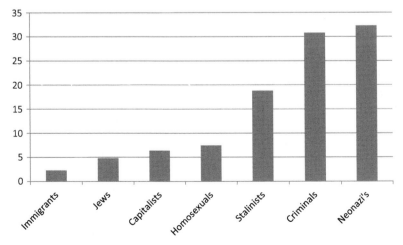

FIGURE 7.2 Disliked groups and their percentages
Adapted from Peffley & Rohrschneider (2003)

58 Part 1 Opposition

themselves that contradicts the first voice. If the one (tolerant) voice speaks up, then they seem not be aware of what the other (intolerant) voice is saying at another moment. The emotional voice ignores the rational voice, and the last voice is not aware of what the first one is saying. For the political scientists Thomassen, Van Ham & Andeweg (2014), this was a reason to conclude "It seems that the support for fundamental civil rights in the majority of the population is no more than a very thin layer of varnish that easily can be scratched away"(p. 103).

These findings yield to the insight that it is important that people become aware of their own emotions. This can occur by giving attention to one's own feelings of aversion or antipathy toward other individuals or certain groups of a population. We should become aware of our responses to certain characteristics of individuals and groups in society, and acknowledge our own emotions that are provoked by those individuals. Such responses can be strong and deeply felt, but they can also be very subtle and hardly noticeable. Particularly in the latter case, it is important to develop sensitivity to your own emotions and to realize that our primary responses toward strangers often reflect intolerance instead of tolerance. The question then is not: How can we suppress or deny intolerance?, but: How can we acknowledge intolerance and provide a reasonable response to it? From a democratic point of view, it is useful to accept our natural inclination to be intolerant towards strangers or groups that we don't know. The problem lies not in the experience of intolerance itself, but in the *lack of awareness* of it. Only when we are aware of our intolerance, are we able to give an appropriate response to it and come up with alternative possibilities.

To give a "democratic response" to our natural intolerance, it is essential to consider these feelings from the perspective of our reasoning. Only when we are conscious of our emotions of intolerance, can we realize that this can conflict with what we prefer on the basis of our reasoning capacities. At that moment we see a dialogical relationship between emotional positioning ("Emotionally I feel the urge to act in such-and-such a way") and the counter-positioning of reasoning ("From the perspective of my reason I want to assume a different position"). At the interface between emotion and reason there arises a dialogical contradiction that might lead to considerations other than just purely following our primary emotions. Only when this happens can the ubiquitous phenomenon that "only the other person is intolerant, not me," be corrected.

The reason–emotion dialogue also has the potential to function as an adequate response to the tendency of some people to "compartmentalize" their emotions of intolerance, indignation, or anger. Compartmentalization is basically an internal process of putting our feelings toward someone, or some experience, in a metaphorical box and putting them on a shelf in the back of our mind to be forgotten, or stirred up only when something reminds us they're there (Weishar, 2018). Compartmentalization is not necessarily a negative emotional reaction. Some people use it to protect their inner self against other contradictory or conflicting emotions. However, an over-use of compartmentalization would have the disadvantage that some emotions are excluded from change. Indeed, the reason–emotion dialogue can only function adequately when we have an open mind, also to ourselves.

Summarizing

- Our reason does not stand above our emotions, but they stand next to each other. They require each other.
- Emotions that are often labelled as negative are not by definition undesirable. They can function as a source of adaptive and constructive behavior.
- Emotional responses occur faster than responses based on reason, but can eventually lead to an inner dialogue between emotion and reason.
- Paying attention enhances our sensitivity to our emotional responses.
- We notice a contradiction between our emotional intolerance and our reason. This requires that we pay attention to our emotions and activate a constructive counter-position from our reason.

Critical Questions

There seems to be a contradiction in the text. Earlier in this chapter we saw that emotion and reason exist alongside each other: If people are motivated only by their reasoning capacities, it would be difficult to make decisions because they would be reasoning endlessly before coming to a conclusion. In some cases it would be better to listen to our emotions because that would give us information about our preferences. Later in the text, it is explained that we experience rather intolerant emotions about groups of people we do not like very much. And that is not consistent with our "democratic reasoning."

- What is your opinion on this contradiction?
- Or is there no contradiction at all, and it only appears to be so?

For centuries it was assumed, at least in philosophy circles, that reason is superior and stands above emotion. Nowadays we think that reason and emotion stand next to each other, and that these two faculties allow for a dialogical relationship with each other.

- If that is the case, does this mean that reason and emotion are equivalent? Or is one more important than the other? What are your thoughts about this?
- Did you detect other possible contradictions in the text? Or non-explicit presuppositions?

Exercise

Study the picture in Figure 7.3 and try to answer the following questions (it doesn't matter in what sequence you answer the questions).

- What do you feel when you look at this picture?
- What exactly do you see in this picture? Try to be neutral and factual in your description, without any prejudicial interpretation, judgment, etc.
- What do you think is happening here?
- What is your opinion about what you are seeing in this picture? What *I*-position does this evoke? What reasons can you give for your opinion?

When you have answered these questions, start a discussion with the other people in your group. First share your answers with the other group members.

- Did you succeed in describing in a factual manner what you saw in the picture?
- How do you describe this picture based on your feelings about it? And how do you describe this picture based on your reasoning? Do your reason and emotion invoke different responses or do they coincide?

FIGURE 7.3 *This is what we die for*
Source: Amnesty International (2016, p. 22).

On the website of Amnesty International[3] you will find a story about the origin of the picture. There you can also find a supplementary exercise for this chapter.

Reflecting

In "From Your Own Experience" you have explored to what extent emotion and reason play a role in your points of view. Can you now go further in this exploration? Are you still thinking in the same way? Did your viewpoint become stronger, or did it change?

Can you, at the end of this chapter, answer the following questions?

- Can you mention *one* opinion about yourself that is largely influenced by your emotion?
- Can you mention *one* opinion about yourself that is largely influenced by your reason?
- If some of your opinions are partly influenced by your emotions, do you think that those opinions are also influenced by your reasoning?
- Have you ever done or experienced something in which you could bring emotion and reason into dialogue with each other? Can you describe this in some sentences?

Notes

1. A similar procedure in which conscious and unconscious *I*-positions can be harmonized is the Composition Method (Hermans & Hermans-Konopka, 2010; Konopka & van Beers, 2014). In this method, people are invited to create an artistic composition of their personal identity by placing little rocks of different forms, colors, and sizes in various spatial formations.
2. However, we need to mention here that, more recently, the number of "illiberal" democracies (so-called democracies in name, but with autocratic leaders) that limit the rights of minorities has also risen, as in Russia, Turkey, and Hungary. See also the international survey by the Pew Research Center (Kent, 2019) showing that in many countries people were more dissatisfied than satisfied with the way democracy is working (see the Introduction to this book).
3. https://www.amnesty.org/en/documents/afr62/3183/2016/en/

EPILOGUE TO PART 1

In Part 1, focusing on opposition, we proceeded from various basic premises. A human being is not just a one-dimensional entity. Like a diamond we exhibit several facets, and we call those *I*-positions. An *I*-position is a part of yourself that stands in relation to other persons in the social environment. In relation to other people we can distinguish positions like I as a brother, I as a daughter, I as a friend, I as a counselor, etc. We can also define *I*-positions according to a position we occupy in society: I as a student, I as a consumer, I as a citizen. There are also *I*-positions in relation to the other positions in our inner self, for example, I as critical about my eating behavior, or I as controlling myself when I'm angry.

In a democracy, it is very important that there is room for opposition. This requires *dialogue* about our own values and considerations, and those of other people. In sharing opposing viewpoints, we come to know each other by paying attention to other views that may be different from ours. And perhaps we can make better decisions when we consider alternative viewpoints that are offered by other people.

In this part of the book we have focused on how a particular *I*-position relates to other *I*-positions in yourself, and how you can begin and maintain a conversation between those *I*-positions. For example, we have seen how "I as emotional" can be opposed to "I as reasonable" and how a dialogue between those two modalities is needed to arrive at a reconciliation. In itself, this is an illustration of democracy or, more specifically, inner democracy, as this conversation takes place within yourself.

For a good conversation, either with other people or between the different *I*-positions within yourself, a certain degree of *flexibility* is required. The three-step model is a way to achieve this flexibility. When you use that model in a conversation, you are trying explicitly to give space to other opinions from partners in the conversation. And that same process occurs in yourself in regard to conflicting positions within yourself. Therefore it is necessary that you can assume

Epilogue to Part 1 **63**

a *meta-position*. The conversation between multiple *I*-positions takes place from a meta-position. In Chapter 5 about meta-positions we discussed the conversation between I as a consumer and I as a citizen. Those two *I*-positions often have an antagonistic relationship. However, you are able to look at this antagonism from the perspective of a meta-position. This is what we mean when we refer to inner democracy: Having a conversation within yourself in which you are able to assume a view as from a high-flying helicopter.

What else is needed for the explanation of inner democracy and its role in democracy at large? In the first place, we need to control our urge to immediately express our opinion about certain topics. We suggest, listen first and ask yourself if you understand what the other person is saying. *Suspension of judgment* also means the suspension of certainty. We should allow for a certain level of *uncertainty*, because only then can something new arise in a conversation with another person, such as new insights, or new behavioral choices. And we should not forget the role of *emotions*. Emotions can function as good advisors because they can point you, for example, to injustices: "I feel this is not right, this is not fair." Emotion and reasoning function as two powerful *I*-positions in yourself, and you will need to bring those positions in contact with each other. That can be very helpful to yourself in your thoughts and behavior, because it tells you how your viewpoints are being invoked by your emotions, or by your reasoning, or by a productive combination of them.

Self-Quiz for Part 1

To strengthen your memory storage of what you have learned so far, at the end of each Part you will find a self-quiz consisting of 10 multiple-choice questions to check if you have correctly digested the background information. To pass the quiz, you need to give at least 7 correct answers to the 10 questions. If you do not pass the test, you are invited to re-examine the chapters of that Part and answer the quiz questions again. The correct answers are included in the Appendix at the end of the book. This method ensures that you get specific feedback about the level of your knowledge regarding a certain topic, and that you have mastered the content of the chapters.

Each question has four alternative answers. For each question there is only one correct or best answer. Select just one answer to each question.

1. To develop alternative viewpoints in conversations with other people, we have to use a flexible position-repertoire. To succeed in this undertaking, we have to find a balance between:

   a   open and closed boundaries of our *I*-positions
   b   soft and rigid boundaries of our *I*-positions
   c   speaking and active listening
   d   opinions and viewpoints

64 Part 1 Opposition

2. According to Bohm, in order to suspend your judgment you have to pay attention to:

   a the emotions of the other person
   b the emotions of the other person and your own emotions
   c the body language of the other person
   d attentive listening

3. What is a better alternative to the question: "What do you think about this?"

   a What actually do you know about this?
   b What actually are your reasons for your opinion?
   c How can we understand this?
   d How different is your opinion from mine?

4. The three-step model makes use of changing perspectives in a flexible way. Can you identify those three steps?

   a 1. taking up a position and expressing it;
     2. the other person listens and responds to this;
     3. moving back to position 1 and mixing in elements of the other person's opinion
   b 1. listening to another person;
     2. expressing your opinion on the basis of the first opinion;
     3. the other person responds to this
   c 1. adopting a position and expressing it;
     2. the other person adopts a contrary position;
     3. reaching a synthesis between the two viewpoints
   d 1. listening to another person;
     2. asking for clarification;
     3. formulating your own opinion

5. What are the four characteristics of a meta-position?

   a taking distance–overview–cause–effect
   b taking distance–overview–history–future
   c taking distance–overview–insight–synthesis
   d taking distance–overview–reason–emotion

6. Solomon was, just like many other people then and now, very capable of giving other people advice, but he could not apply this wisdom in his own life. What is the underlying cause of this problem?

   a people cannot think very clearly about themselves
   b people do not know very well which *I*-positions are playing a role
   c people express their opinions too quickly
   d people cannot distance themselves from their own emotions

Epilogue to Part 1   **65**

7. People can use four strategies to reduce high levels of uncertainty. Which of the four statements below does *not* apply to this?

   a   considerably reducing the number and variations of I-positions
   b   paying attention to the body language and facial expressions of other persons
   c   giving the leading role to *one* I-position
   d   forming rigid boundaries between "we" and "they"

8. In uncertain situations, it is good for the development of inner democracy to admit uncertainty in yourself. Which of the capacities mentioned below can be helpful and might offer the possibility of dealing in with uncertainty a constructive way?

   a   being able to make a distinction between facts and opinions
   b   being able to reduce the number and variations of I-positions
   c   taking up a (preferably multiple) meta-position
   d   acknowledging the value of "negative" emotions

9. What is the merit of "negative" emotions (e.g., anxiety, guilty feelings)?

   a   they motivate us to undertake an action plan
   b   they stimulate awareness of the value of positive emotions
   c   they can lead to exploration
   d   they offer us the possibility to empathize with the experiential world of another person

10. What is the best way to react to our own intolerance?

   a   acknowledging and accepting that a certain amount of intolerance is unavoidable
   b   acknowledging this and trying to find an appropriate answer to it
   c   acknowledging this and finding out how and why it is happening
   d   acknowledging this and correcting your own intolerance

PART 2

Cooperation

8

LEARNING FROM YOURSELF

Learning from each other also means learning from the dialogue between various *I*-positions in yourself. In this first chapter of Part 2 we will describe three of these dialogs: Coming to an agreement with yourself; consulting yourself; and criticizing yourself.

From Your Own Experience

Do you remember a situation where you had to come to terms with yourself? For example, making a deal with yourself? For instance, in a situation where you wanted to change your behavior? Can you describe that experience: What was it all about? What did it involve? After you have written down a few sentences about this experience, it might be interesting to ask yourself: "Why did I actually have to come to terms with myself? Was there no other way to handle this situation? Which *I*-positions were involved in this particular situation? What was eventually the result of this agreement I made with myself?" Write down your experiences in a few statements.

Background Information

There are several ways you can learn from *I*-positions in yourself that closely resemble the way you relate to other people. We will describe three different forms in this process: Coming to an agreement with yourself; consulting yourself; and developing constructive criticisms of yourself.

First, *coming to an agreement with yourself*. We form agreements with other people, and with ourselves, with the unspoken promise that we will follow up on them. This can vary from agreeing to take a new initiative to stopping

70 Part 2 Cooperation

a bad habit. For our concept of inner democracy, we also need to keep our agreements. You can come to an agreement with yourself with the intention that you will keep to it. For example, I can decide to undertake some physical exercise, or a sport, or I can decide to restrict myself from eating things that are delicious but unhealthy. Or I can come to an agreement with myself that after a certain time in the evening I will no longer look at my mobile devices.

Second, *consulting yourself.* In our everyday life it can happen that we consult an expert for advice about an issue that we cannot solve ourselves. Just as when you consult another person and ask them for advice, you can also consult yourself. You address another person or yourself to get a relevant answer to your question. Sometimes you can address yourself with an important question to which you have no immediate answer. Self-consultation occurs typically in situations where you have to make an important decision. In that case, you invoke a specific *I*-position in yourself that you ask for advice. Here are some examples: "Shall I apply for that job or not?" "Shall I attend that school or not?" "Shall I continue with that contact or end it?" "Shall I accept that invitation or not?" You then need time to "walk around" with that question. Some individuals do this by taking their dog out for a walk, others by listening to soothing music, or "sleeping on it." You then wait for a good quality answer before you decide what to do.

This process of self-consultation is not just restricted to conscious processes in our mind. You might go to sleep with an important question on your mind and it can happen that you wake up with the right answer. Our minds need time, at a lower level of our consciousness, to gather information and make connections to find a fitting answer. It can also happen that, when talking with somebody else, your partner in the conversation mentions something and you realize: "That's it!" On a lower level of consciousness there was already something present but still rather dormant, and waiting for your partner's remark in the conversation triggers the response: "That's it!" "That is what I need to do!"

Third, *developing constructive criticisms of yourself.* For example, in our everyday life it is important to develop the critical capacity to make a distinction between news reports that are true and what can be called "fake news." It is also essential to recognize in time if you are dealing with someone who wants to deceive you. But giving self-criticism can go too far. There are "criticasters" who criticize everything they encounter, possibly because they have a hostile attitude toward other people, or because to criticize is for them the only way to sustain a certain feeling of self-esteem. A similar phenomenon can be found in self-criticism. In some cases, self-criticism is healthy and constructive, but in other cases it can be harmful and destructive. Whereas task-oriented self-criticism is generally beneficial, person-oriented self-criticism is often destructive.

Making Agreements with Yourself

The American sociologist Regina Kenen (1984), who studied this phenomenon, devoted special attention to coming to agreements with yourself (e.g. quitting a bad habit, or doing another person a favor). In such cases, a person tries to convince themselves that it is fine to do certain things, but not other things. The convincing position in yourself then involves statements about a particular behavior (e.g., I want to quit smoking). The position that needs to be convinced is the position in you that harbors a bad habit. It is this latter position that determines whether the agreement with yourself will be fulfilled or not. In other words: I let myself be convinced by myself that in the future I will behave in such-and-such manner. If one of the positions in yourself does not like the arrangement (or doesn't agree with it), then nothing will happen. It is futile if the convincing position imposes on the self an unfeasible regime from which it is clear, from the very start, that it will not be successful. The voice in yourself that needs to be convinced might then protest and say things like: "I will not succeed in this," "I know that I can't keep this agreement". *Here we notice an inner dialogue.* There is a convincing position in yourself, and at the same time another position that needs to be convinced. If both positions agree then the result is a resolution that has implications for your future behavior.

On the basis of her study, Kenen draws the conclusion that self-agreements, under the assumption that they are realistic, make it possible for people to control their own behavior. One part of yourself regulates the other part. If it happens in a way you want it to, and you have a good feeling about it, then you will experience more order and consistency in yourself, with the added advantage that you come to notice that you can cooperate well with yourself. In that case there is a good chance that the new behavior will become realized, instead of unilaterally imposing on yourself an iron regime without listening carefully to different *I*-positions in yourself. In the latter case we speak about a monologue instead of a dialogue. The advantage of a dialogical relation with yourself is that the decision is supported by both *I*-positions. A self-agreement should not be confused with a good intention that has a more or less non-obligatory character. A self-agreement is the result of a thorough dialogue with yourself and reaching a conclusion about what you need to do or not to do. You can consider the successes and failures on the path to self-agreement as a learning process, in the sense of learning from yourself.

Self-consultation

It is not just our unconscious processes that operate with self-consultation. The unconscious process only gives an answer after you have first asked yourself a question. As Louis Pasteur said: "Fortune favors the prepared mind."[1] You will receive a good answer after you have carefully prepared your question and explicitly addressed the question to yourself. We notice something similar in creative processes: you only get a beautiful idea when you have walked around for a long time with a question that you cannot immediately answer. And in this way a process develops at a subconscious level that, at a certain moment, can lead to an *Aha-Erlebnis* (a "Eureka moment").

Consultancy expert George Lovell (2000) explains that people can develop this process of self-consultancy. He applies this in his own work by first describing to himself *what* he wants to consult himself about. He also notes that it is helpful when you talk to yourself in the third person. So not: "I wonder if …" but: "George wonders if … ." The advantage of this technique is that it creates more distance between the person who is asking the question and the (same) person who answers it. In the terminology of this book, you can say that by using the third-person construction you look at yourself and the problem as if from a meta-position. Then, thanks to the increased distance, the opportunity arises for more than one *I*-position to get involved in the process (think back about the "multiple meta-positions" discussed in Part 1).

Lovell emphasizes that a certain degree of receptivity is necessary to facilitate self-consultation. Just as you open yourself up to the advice of an expert, so you can open yourself up to receive the right counsel. We can't expect to receive a valuable answer as a result of an impatient or hasty effort to get a quick answer. An enforced answer will not have the same quality as if you have waited a little while and carefully thought about the response you would like to receive. It is necessary to slow the process down, let it take its own time and develop

FIGURE 8.1 Moments of self-consultation
Source: Wikimedia Commons

gradually. Self-consultation therefore requires that you insert a moment or period of silence.[2] When you delve into something and the question is clear, then you have to stop this process for a little while and start doing something else: wandering around, eating, taking a shower, sleeping—and then, suddenly, there is the answer. One of the characteristics of a "good dialogue" is giving space to yourself to ask a good question and wait for a good answer. That is a moment in which you can learn from yourself, and thereby teach yourself.

Self-criticism

Already at the beginning of the 20th century, the influential philosopher and pedagogue John Dewey (1910) pointed out the enormous importance of critical thinking. According to Dewey, this is a necessary capacity that is important for both students and society, as well as for democracy. He emphasizes that critical thinking is needed for the construction of ideas that can guide human behavior. Critical thinking is essential for the development of our intellectual capacities in the form of questions and answers. Dewey emphasizes that each student needs to construct their own knowledge, not as a learning process that is given by someone from the outside and then rehearsed, but as a personal learning process. Students develop their own intellectual capacities by paying attention to new developments, making themselves familiar with them, and then reflecting on them in a critical way.

Canadian psychologist Mark Lewis (2002) described how we often use short statements to evaluate our own functioning, like "bad!," "stupid!," "worthless!," or at best "alright!," "very good!," "wonderful!," "yes!" Such inner evaluations result from many of our behavioral acts that indicate some form of achievement. These are normal ways of evaluation and self-correction that can be helpful for improving our behavioral acts and skills. They can be part of inner dialogs that have the character of self-encouragement and self-correction (Brinthaupt & Dove, 2012). Along the path of self-correction we can learn from our inner dialogues.

However, self-criticism can also result in a process of critical self-evaluation in which people continuously develop negative thoughts and feelings about themselves. The negative evaluation doesn't relate to a specific behavior and is not transient in nature, but stretches over different situations and applies even to the person as a whole. Eventually, a person might come to experience him or herself as "worthless" or "inferior." As part of his research, Whelton (2001) asked students who suffered from depression to imagine a situation in which they had failed. It then appeared that these students felt more contempt for themselves, felt more shameful about themselves, were less assertive, and were more submissive in comparison to students who had less depressive feelings. It appears that critical self-evaluation in depressive people is broader, more intense, and directed more at the entire person than in individuals who do not have those stark feelings of depression.

So we can conclude that self-criticism is not in and of itself good or bad, and is not necessarily disadvantageous for a person's well-being. It depends on the intensity, frequency, and emotional quality (being happy or feeling depressed). It also depends on the situation in which the criticism occurs. If the situation involves a certain task but you do not achieve a certain goal, then self-criticism can motivate someone to refine their own capabilities and urge themselves to do better the next time. If, however, in almost all situations you have the feeling "I am not okay about the way I feel at this moment," then self-criticism can have a strong obstructing influence not only on the level of your achievements, but also on your overall feeling of self-esteem.

In this chapter we have discussed three phenomena that can help us in learning from ourselves: *self-agreement, self-consultation,* and *self-criticism.* You can also turn the sequence around. At the right moment and in the right situation, you can turn to task-related self-criticism. If your self-criticism is related to performing a task more or less well, then this can be helpful for further developing your capacities. If, however, self-criticism is directed at yourself in an over-generalizing way and leads to feelings of self-blame, then this can be counter-productive. From a task-oriented self-criticism, you can consult yourself to find a way to improve yourself. In this phase, you open yourself up and listen to your own thoughts and feelings, which can be used as a guideline in adjusting your behavior. And finally, you can make agreements with yourself to realize your goals. These self-agreements are important to determine a direction for your actions and protect yourself against too much distraction.

FIGURE 8.2 Task-related self-criticism improves your performance
Source: Wikimedia Commons

Summarizing

- To give you a first impression of what it means to learn from yourself, we have described three ways of learning: self-agreement, self-consultation, and self-criticism.
- Self-agreements happen after an inner dialogue between two *I*-positions: one that is proposing the agreement, and the other that is accepting the proposal. You have to be able to work *with* yourself, rather than dictate to yourself, in order to make realistic agreements.
- Self-consultation takes place when you have to make important decisions: You consult yourself. Good advice is often the result of processes that are not yet conscious, but you may become aware of these processes at a later time.
- Self-criticism works best when it is task-oriented and constructive, and when it is dependent on the specific task you are undertaking.

Critical Questions

- Why do people have agreements with themselves? Or can they only make agreements with other people?
- And what about self-consultation? If our unconscious plays such an important role in this process, how can you then still influence this process in a conscious way? Sometimes it might be better to consult another person when confronted with important decisions. Do you agree or disagree?
- If perhaps self-criticism can be threatening to your personal feeling of self-esteem, wouldn't it be better to *always* think about yourself positively, if you could (?), and ban all negative thoughts about yourself?

Exercises

Excercise 1

Self-agreement

What are you going to do when you make a—good—agreement with another person? Engage in a short Socratic conversation with some fellow students about good agreements.

In a productive conversation, reflect with other people on something that you have experienced. In this case we are talking about making a *good* agreement. One of you tells the others about a good agreement that they made not so long ago with someone else. Try to describe the situation in a clear and lively way. The other students can ask questions for clarification.

Afterwards, you are going to have a conversation with each other in your group. So, what makes this a *good* agreement? Think about the process, and its

76 Part 2 Cooperation

result, to identify the aspects that were instrumental in thinking about this example as a good agreement.

When you have finished this task and made a short list of the aspects you identified, discuss with each other the following question: Are these then the characteristics of a *good* agreement? Often that is the case. But more often you might think, something may be missing here. What features do you think we are missing?

In summary:

1. Describe an example of a *good* agreement.
2. Ask for clarification.
3. Identify the features that make this example a *good* agreement.
4. Discuss those features: What do they contribute to making this a *good* agreement?
5. Review the characteristics and features that contribute to a good agreement. Is this sufficient or do we need to add something more to it?

You have now established the characteristics of a good agreement. Apply these characteristics to an agreement you have made with yourself (e.g., the self-agreement you had in mind at the beginning of this chapter). Now, was this a good agreement with yourself? Why, or why not? Share this with your fellow students.

Exercise 2

Self-consultation

This exercise is a variant of the exercise in Chapter 5. If you completed that exercise, then you have given a short description of yourself from the point of view of an (imaginary) third person. You have also described a difficult situation, and that imaginary other person has given you advice about it, unasked. You can use the notes of that exercise to continue further with this exercise (but you can do this exercise independently of the previous one).

1. Zoom in on a problem or a difficult situation with which you are confronted, for example, a conflict in which you are involved, or a difficult choice you have to make.
2. Which of your *I*-positions are involved in this?
3. Describe the problem from a third person's viewpoint as if someone else is describing it; it is important for the exercise that you continue to keep describing the problem in this mode.[NAME] is … (short description of you, yourself). He or she has recently experienced the following: "He/she … " Describe what you think happened to him or her emotionally. How did

this happen? (the why-question, or the how-did-this-come-about-question).

Then formulate the question to ask for advice from this third person. Try to formulate the question as carefully and clearly as possible: The question to [NAME] is: ...

Now consult yourself and give advice to yourself! It is wise to first start a conversation with yourself in which you can describe your initial advice. Afterwards you can think of different advice from different *I*-positions, or from other persons. Which other *I*-position or other person would you choose? What advice would they give? Keep asking yourself: Could other advice be given by other *I*-positions?

Exercise 3

Self-criticism

Do you ever think in negative terms about yourself or about your behavior? Saying "no" to this question would be very remarkable! Recall the different possibilities. Self-criticism can be undermining for your feelings of self-esteem if you direct it to yourself as a person. However, it can be very constructive if your self-criticism is specific and task-oriented. This means that you need to transform self-criticism from person-oriented to task-oriented or situation-oriented. Self-criticism such as: "I'm always shy in company" is not very productive. Transformed into situation-oriented self-criticism, it could be: "During school breaks I have difficulty making good contact with other people."

The exercise here is: Can you transform personal self-criticism into task-oriented self-criticism? Now convert the expressions of self-criticism below, that are oriented toward the person, into expressions that are more task-oriented:

- "I am a dreamer, and that is why I will not succeed in my chosen field of study."
- "I cannot deal very well with situations in which I lose."
- "I am not attractive to other people."
- "I cannot and dare not disagree with my parents."
- "After all, I'm not a very creative person."

Many of us think about ourselves in these types of terms—most of us sometimes have personally self-directed criticisms. Do you sometimes use this method? Which expressions do you use? Can you translate your personal expressions into more task-oriented self-criticisms? And when you have done so, what advice would you give yourself (self-consultation)?

Reflecting

- By now you have gained more insight into the various *I*-positions you can assume. Can you also take up a meta-position (looking from "above")? If you need to, you can look again at Chapter 5).
- Can you now, from a meta-position like this, make a list of points you think you need for making an agreement with yourself? Why do you think it is necessary to do so?
- Are you critical about certain aspects of yourself? Do you want to consult yourself about some of the points on your list?
- Can you apply the insights you have acquired to make a good agreement in a dialogue with yourself, and to make a good self-agreement? Also, check out if these insights might help you, or if they still seem to fall short. What can you do to conduct a better dialogue with yourself in this self-agreement?
- Now go back to what you have said in "From Your Own Experience." Do you want to change something in your initial formulations about your agreements with yourself? What have you learned from this chapter?

Notes

1. Louis Pasteur, inaugural address, Faculté des Sciences, Lille, December 7, 1854.
2. See Hermans & Hermans-Konopka (2010, pp. 174–190) for the characteristics of "good dialogue". For dialogue and education in a racial and cultural context, see Fecho (2004). For dialogical self and teacher identity, see Monereo (2019). Concerning the relation between silence and dialogue, see Lehmann, Kardum & Klempe (2019).

9

THE POWER OF LISTENING

To know something about somebody else and to understand another person, we need to listen. Listening helps us to understand the other person. However, listening not only benefits the listener, but is also very important for the person to whom we are listening. In this chapter we discuss the meaning of the power of listening, specifically high-quality listening.

From Your Own Experience

We all have experienced occasionally telling something to another person and then thinking: They have indeed heard me, but have they listened to me? What exactly is the difference: What have they done, or neglected to do, that makes you ask if they have listened to you? Why do you appreciate it if somebody has listened to you very well? Are you, yourself, someone who can listen well? Can you give an example of listening to somebody very well? What was the effect on the other person? Please try to formulate your answers to these questions in a few statements.

Background Information

Sometimes we try to convince another person by providing arguments. When we engage in a discussion we often try to convince the other person of our views by adding statements such as: "This is true because … " Or, "This is not true because … ." The other person can react to this with a counter-argument. Via a process of argument and counter-argument, one of the parties can appear as the "winner." There is also the possibility that both participants come to a conclusion that they both agree on.

80 Part 2 Cooperation

However, it is not always a very effective method to try to convince someone through argument. If a speaker realizes they are confronted with a counter-argument, they can experience it as a violation of their own right to cherish their own opinion. The counter-argument then is experienced as threatening because it is at the expense of the self-esteem of the speaker. The speaker may get defensive and adopt a "hedgehog" stance. The result is that the partner in the conversation is going to strengthen their initial position. But that is contrary to what you are trying to accomplish, namely that the speaker yields to the power of your arguments. The result is a "boomerang effect:" Your conversation partner does not open him or herself self up to your arguments, but instead rejects them. The boomerang effect then gets stronger: The opposing person is also going to use arguments that you yourself would reject.

Objective and Subjective Ambivalence

Is it possible to change someone else's point of view without using any counter-arguments? A group of Israeli researchers (Itzchakov, Kluger & Castro, 2017) wanted to know the effect of actively listening to somebody who gives their opinion about a morally disputed topic. Active listening implies suspending your own judgments, paying close attention to the body language of the other person as well as yourself, identifying their emotions, and especially trying to paraphrase what the other person is saying. The researchers invited their research subjects to give their opinions about moral issues such as organ donation and euthanasia. Their motive was to find out what would happen if trained listeners just listened carefully to a speaker without any counter-reasoning. The researchers suspected that good listening without giving comments would give the other person the space to react to their own contradictions.

The researchers were inspired by the famous psychotherapist Carl Rogers (1951), who is sometimes referred to as "the best listener in the world" and who knew what listening can bring about in the mind of the person who is speaking. Through active listening, an atmosphere of security arises wherein the boundaries of the speakers' selves become more open. The speaker opens up, will be less defensive, and will pay more attention to their own inner contradictions. They start by exploring their own experiences and then discover that their prejudices and generalizations are not completely accurate and, as a result, they start to correct or question such prejudices and generalizations. They discover in themselves opinions and views that conflict with the generalizations on which they had based their initial point of view, and they are then inclined to correct those views in a critical way.

To really fathom the nature of inner contradiction, Itzshakov and colleagues made a distinction between two kinds of contradiction. Here we want to

FIGURE 9.1 Active listening requires full attention
Source: Wikimedia Commons

emphasize this distinction because it is an important element in promoting inner democracy. The first kind is *objective ambivalence*, meaning that someone can simultaneously entertain positive as well as negative thoughts or feelings about a certain issue, and that they are not standing in each other's way. For example, you can say: "On the one hand I appreciate that he … ; on the other hand I have difficulty with how … ." In this case you notice two real (objective) aspects of something or someone that are in conflict with each other. At the same time, you are able to face that contradiction without immediately abandoning one or another aspect. You are permitting both aspects to play a role in the eventual outcome. The second form of contradiction is called *subjective ambivalence*. This refers to an experience of confusion and a feeling of being torn inside. In that case you might say: "I feel confused, I don't know what I want" or "I want it, but at the same time I don't want it, I can't make up my mind, it's a mess." This happens when we can't organize our thoughts and feelings well and, as a result, they stumble over each other and get mixed up. The distinction between objective and subjective ambivalence is important because it explains why objective ambivalence is needed for a well thought-out judgment. Subjective ambivalence, however, is something most people want to avoid or want to reject outright, because it confuses them and makes it hard to reach unequivocal decisions.

Good Listening Stimulates Depolarization

After the researchers had described this distinction, they went a step further in their explorations. They wanted to know the effect of active listening on the

82 Part 2 Cooperation

subjective and active ambivalence of the person to whom they were listening. If trained investigators listened to the subjects of the experiment in an empathic, non-judgmental, accepting, and respectful way ("high-quality listening"), then it turned out that the speakers in that situation experienced less social anxiety and were less defensive. They also experienced more objective ambivalence, in contrast to a situation where the listeners assumed a less interested role and reacted in a distracted way ("low-quality listening"). This increase of objective ambivalence was *not* associated with an increase in subjective ambivalence. In other words, via high-quality listening the speakers were able to distinguish different sides of a topic without becoming confused.

But something more was going on. The researchers discovered that under the influence of high-quality listening, people's opinions about euthanasia and organ donation became less extreme. This is an indication that this mode of listening has a depolarizing effect, something that was not very discernible with low-quality listening. The favorable effect could not be ascribed to listening per se, but to *active* (high-quality) listening. Apparently, active listening creates more space in the self of an individual for tolerating inner contradictions. This tolerance then has a depolarizing effect. Even though the speakers did not change their opinion from "for" to "against," or vice versa, their opinions became less extreme, meaning that the speakers were less radical in rejecting opinions that differed from their own.

Contradiction and Inner Democracy

To promote inner democracy, it is important to realize that the absence of any form of inner conflict or contradiction results in polarizing processes having free play, not being countered by an opposing force in a person's self. Tolerating or stimulating inner contradiction, especially in the form of objective ambivalence, has the potential to let counter-forces arise in the self. For the emergence of such counter-forces, rational counter-arguments brought forward by someone else are not needed.

The advantage of stimulating inner contradiction is it generates more space for the inner opponent, as we discussed in Part 1 of this book. If this opponent gets access to the inner self and is given the opportunity to play a role in an inner dialogue, then an important condition is created for a democratic learning process. In such a process, the contradictory *I*-positions can influence each other and learn from each other. Contradiction and conflicts, and tolerance for them, are important not only for inner democracy, but also for democracy at large. Political groups can work together only if they are willing to listen to their opponents and acknowledge contradictory positions and viewpoints. Then they can work together more usefully, settle for compromises, and reach a decision and agreement. If those groups do not listen to each other, do not tolerate each other's point of view, or even consider the other group as an enemy, then the chances are high

The Power of Listening **83**

that we end up in a fruitless polarizing process in which no mutual decisions based on shared interests can be reached.

The research discussed here demonstrates that we can allow conflicting feelings and beliefs to play a role in the realm of our inner democracy. Active listening creates space for tolerating inner speech, and particularly contradictory speech. And this space is necessary for the development of inner democracy as a learning process. This doesn't mean that arguments and reasons are not desirable when you are involved in a discussion with other people. It just means that there should be moments of active listening when you are in conversations with others, even with people you disagree with (although this might be quite difficult to accomplish).

Summarizing

- A counter-argument can be experienced as threatening, with the result that the speaker becomes defensive.
- This defensive attitude is weakened when you use an "active listening" mode: Being empathetic, non-judgmental, and respectful.
- Active listening fosters objective ambivalence: Being able to make a clear and concise distinction between contradictory viewpoints, and trying not to become confused by them.
- Active listening fosters depolarization, even in regard to topics that have a serious moral impact.

Critical Questions

In this text we encountered the following premise: If one practices active listening, then people will nuance their opinions (i.e., acknowledge contradictions), and those opinions then also become less extreme.

There is a caveat here. Does this imply that if people express reprehensible ideas, you should then especially pay attention to them? And not make too many objections because that may function only as a boomerang?

Exercise

This exercise resembles the one in Chapter 3. In that chapter we discussed suspending judgment. In the exercise with a narrator and a questioner, the questioners were not allowed to express what they thought about the narrator's ideas. We are repeating this exercise here, but now we are paying special attention to the listening attitude. The questioner from the previous exercise is now the listener.

84 Part 2 Cooperation

The exercise involves three people. There are three roles: a speaker; a listener; and an observer. The exercise takes five minutes, and afterward you discuss the observations of the observer.

- The *speaker* holds a clear and distinct position in relation to a theme or topic, or something they have recently experienced. Choose something that made a big impression on you, something that made you angry, sad, or happy. Choose a theme that you can discuss in a very animated way. The exercise doesn't work if you are finished talking after just a minute! Start by formulating your own position in *one* sentence, and then explain what it's all about and why you hold this viewpoint. Go ahead!
- The task of the *listener* is to listen actively. This means:
  - don't display your opinions or thoughts about the position of the speaker, you are just trying to understand the position of the other person;
  - pay special attention to your own body language and body posture;
  - assume a relaxed position (don't exaggerate, though) while focusing on the other person;
  - look the other person in the eye as much as possible;
  - nod once in a while;
  - once in a while insert some silent moments;
  - only ask questions for clarification: "What do you mean by ... ?," "Do I understand you correctly when you say that ... ," etc.
  - once in a while, summarize what has been said in the conversation by using the same words as the speaker as much as possible (paraphrasing is something you do in question form: "Do I understand you correctly, if ... ").
- The *observer*, a third person, watches both the narrator and the listener: What do you observe in their use of language, their pose of certainty, body language, facial expressions? How do you interpret those?

After five minutes, both the listener and the speaker are going to discuss their experiences in response to the observations of the observer. Central to this follow-up discussion is the listening attitude of the listener and the effect it had on the speaker and their opinions:

- Was there an atmosphere of safety, protection, and acceptance?
- How did the opinions of the speaker develop? Did their opinions change during the conversation, and in what way? Did you detect an objective ambivalence? Or could you notice also a subjective ambivalence?
- Did you notice any influence of the listener's attitude on the speaker's point of view?

We advise you to do this exercise at least once more, with each person assigned a different role. Listening requires exercise.

Reflecting

- What do you think is the importance of active listening?
- Do you think of yourself as a good listener?
- Compare your answers with the answers you wrote down earlier in the section: "From Your Own Experience." Do you have some other suggestions that would make you a better listener?

10

WHEN VALUES MATTER

Often we think that a judgment is based on knowledge and rational considerations. However, this is only partly true. Many of our opinions and viewpoints, certainly when it concerns moral issues, are provoked by our intuitions and emotions. In this chapter we invite you to reflect on your own moral positions, and we will discuss how to deal with those.

From Your Own Experience

What are moral issues, according to you? Can you give some examples? What makes these issues *moral*? Do you have distinct opinions or ideas about this subject? Write them down. Can you provide some reasons for your opinions and ideas?

Background Information

We often think that we need knowledge about a certain issue before we can give an informed judgment about it. Knowledge seems to come before judgment. At the same time, we assume that when somebody has no knowledge about a certain issue, then they cannot give a rational judgment about that topic, and then they would be wise not to air an opinion. However, there is a lot of evidence that these assumptions are often ignored.

No Knowledge, But Still a Judgment

Let's take a look at a recent technological development, nanotechnology. We have chosen this example to demonstrate how people react to issues about which they have no, or very little, knowledge. Nanoparticles are ultra-small particles on a scale of a billionth of a meter. This technology is leading to new applications such as food containers that kill bacteria, stain-resistant clothing, effective skincare products, smaller and faster computers, and other applications. Nanotechnology is controversial because there is some evidence that exposure to those ultra-small particles (e.g., inhaling them) can have harmful effects on our health (Arora, Rajwade & Paknikar, 2012).

Researcher Dan Kahan and his team (Braman et al., 2007) from Yale University in the USA came up with the idea of asking a group of more than a thousand research subjects what they thought about the pro's and con's of nanotechnology. Before they asked this question, they asked their subjects about their *knowledge* of this technology. It then turned out that 81 percent of the subjects knew hardly anything at all about this specific technology. When the researchers afterwards asked the subjects about their *opinion*, it appeared that as many as 90 percent of the subjects offered an opinion about nanotechnology. Apparently, a vast majority of the subjects were willing to give an opinion about a complex technology without any knowledge of it.

You could ask if it would make a difference if we were to give the research subjects information about this technology. If we gave people who knew nothing about nanotechnology information about it, would this then change their opinion? To be able to answer this question, the researchers gave information about the pros and cons to *one* group but not to the other group (both groups had no knowledge whatsoever about nanotechnology). The researchers gave to the informed group a balanced and neutral overview of the pros and cons of

FIGURE 10.1 Do we use existing knowledge or not?
Source: Wikimedia Commons

88 Part 2 Cooperation

nanotechnology. To the researchers' surprise, it appeared that giving this information hardly made any difference. In the informed group, a slight majority of the subjects saw more pros than cons regarding this technology, but in the group that had not received any information, the percentages were almost the same. The uninformed group had, overall, the same opinion as the informed group. So providing information made little or no difference for assessing the risks of nanotechnology. This result led to the following question: If knowledge and having information about a certain issue make no difference to taking a position, then what is the distinctive factor in this issue?

To answer that question, the researchers made a distinction between different social groups in which people position themselves within society. One group consisted of subjects with a *hierarchical* opinion: they think that in society we should make a distinction between different social classes, religions, races, and genders. They believe that some groups are more valuable than others and consequently should enjoy more privileges. The other group consisted of subjects who had an *egalitarian* view of society. They believe that people should profit equally from the goods of society, regardless of the group to which they belong. It turned out that the subjects in the hierarchical group saw more advantages than risks in the new technology, while for the egalitarian inclined subjects the disadvantages weighted more heavily than the advantages. Apparently, knowledge does not determine a certain position, but the human and world view of the social group to which they believe they belong, does.

The Universal Claim of Moral Positions

Emotionally laden views, especially when they are morally charged, tolerate little or no opposition. When people discuss with each other issues such as cultural diversity, asylum seekers, abortion, euthanasia, climate change, genetic manipulation of food (let alone of embryos), vaccination of children, gay rights, and political beliefs, their positions are often irreconcilably opposed to each other. As soon as people notice fundamental differences between themselves and other people, they either keep on fighting each other, or withdraw behind the walls of their own bastion. The result is that discussions come to a halt and solutions to serious problems remain out of sight.

There is something remarkable about moral opinions: Their universal claim. Suppose someone says: "I value the equality of men and women, but other people do not have to do so," then gender is viewed as a matter of personal taste, comparable with the tolerance one has towards people who prefer pizza over spring rolls. If somebody says: "We in our culture value equality of men and women, but people of other cultures do not have to do so," then they are referring to a social convention that applies to one culture but not the other. However, when gender equality is considered a moral good, and somebody says: "I highly value the equality of men and women, and everyone should think

ALADDIN AND THE WONDERFUL LAMP

Here is a shocking example of judgment without knowledge. In 2015 the American research agency Public Policy Polling asked more than 500 Republican voters about their opinions on political issues. Among other things, they were asked about allowing Muslims into the USA. One question was whether they could agree that Agrabah should be bombed. It turned out that 30 percent supported such a bombing. A majority of 57 percent gave the answer that they were not sure, and just a small minority of 13 percent were against such a bombing. *But* ... Agrabah doesn't exist. It is a fantasy kingdom from the Disney movie *Aladdin* (1992). Just the Arabic sounding name was sufficient to evoke a willingness among the respondents to use violence against a (non-existent) group.

Not only Republicans, but also some Democrats could look back on the research with a blush of shame: 29 percent of them declared that they agreed with such a bombing, while 36 percent were against it.

This research shows that a significant number of participants are willing to take a position and support an action when it concerns groups that evoke negative emotions. Lack of knowledge is not an obstacle. Even far-reaching aggression against a non-existent group becomes possible.

Looking back on their study, the researchers indicated one factor that they thought was determining the responses of their subjects—emotions. They described those emotions as "intuitive responses" that are not informed by knowledge and rational considerations, but are triggered by a first impulse. Subjects gave emotionally laden responses about new technological developments without having a knowledge base for a considered judgment. Once these instantaneous gut responses are established, they are not easy to change, not even if nuanced knowledge is offered about the issue. Subjects are hiding behind the barricades of an emotionally colored position: Here I stand, and here I will stay! The result is a situation of political polarization about the desirability of a particular technology, comparable to the morally tinted controversies around nuclear energy, genetic manipulation, robotics, and global warming. When people hear about such developments, they are inclined to withdraw themselves into their own political camp. They take a polarizing stance towards each other, confirm themselves in their own "perfectly" right position, and consider their own viewpoint as morally superior to others. The individual who holds a different point of view, and thus is an opponent, is perceived as someone who is "wrong" or just "talking nonsense." The point of view of the other must be devalued and, if that is not possible, just ignored. The inner opponent, so much needed for inner democracy, gets no space because the self is "consumed" by an emotion that does not tolerate any opposition.

about this in the same way, also in other cultures," then we are talking about a moral viewpoint. Such a position has a *universal claim* that sets limits on moral diversity and easily leads to intolerance. When somebody says: "I highly value a homosexual marriage, but I have a good friend who considers homosexuality a disease," then one notices raising of eyebrows, instead of acceptance of the fact that people may think differently about such issues.

The universal claim of moral views causes people to shut themselves off from others. We do not allow people who think differently to come too close to ourselves. This was revealed through research by the psychologists Haidt, Rosenberg & Hom (2003), who compared two forms of diversity: *demographic diversity*, such as differences in income and social class; and *moral diversity*, such as differences about abortion and gay rights. When research subjects were asked if they would agree to admitting to college individuals who were different from them, then they said that demographic differences did not bother them. They didn't care much if their fellow-students were rich or poor, or belonged to a different social class. However, they expressed more difficulty in admitting students who held very different views about gay rights or abortion. These differences became even more acute when the researchers asked with whom they wanted to work on a class project. In that case, the students had no difficulty with a fellow student from another income level or social group, but expressed difficulty with a fellow student who thought differently

FIGURE 10.2 Cultural diversity and togetherness
Source: Wikimedia Commons

about abortion or gay rights. The other who is different regarding moral issues has to be kept at a distance.

The Remarkable Absence of the Inner Opponent

In his 2016 book *Waarom iedereen altijd gelijk heeft* [*Why Everyone is Always Right*], the Flemish journalist Ruben Mersch shows, on the basis of a series of studies, that moral views about certain issues often collide head-on and are difficult to change. In a playful summary of his quest, he writes:

> "Entire newspapers are filled daily with tribal disputes. People who are in favor of admitting refugees are, according to their opponents, naïve Islam huggers. The Islam huggers depict their opponents then as heartless individuals. The left blames the right that they only want to give goods to people who already have a lot. The right believes that the left wants to take away their hard-earned money and want to distribute it amongst people who do not want to work for it. Climate alarmists against global warming deniers, people of faith against atheists, green movement supporters against defenders of the industry ... We even fly in each other's hair about the color of the face of Saint Nicholas' little helper.[1] We group ourselves in camps and each camp is convinced that their values and norms are superior. Every attack on our principles we consider as an attack on ourselves."

In many people, we can sense a feeling of "being right" that causes them to take a stand, even about issues of which they have little or no knowledge, as we have seen earlier in this chapter. When we hear about a relatively unknown development (e.g. a new technology or the background of climate change), then our opinion depends more on our already existing views about the society we live in, than on the knowledge we have about the issue in question. The position taken does not follow from rational considerations, but from emotions and intuitions that have been formed often without much thought. Moral opinions and views in particular are firmly anchored in a person's self and very difficult to change. Other or opposing views are considered as not belonging to ourselves, and thus inferior. Moral opinions often have an impervious character, and people are inclined to withdraw themselves from each other and to entrench themselves in their own bastion together with like-minded individuals. In such situations, people put each other in prison-like categories with closed-off walls, with little empathy for the individuals who are located on the other side.

Summarizing

- People often take a position on issues without any knowledge about those issues.
- Positions taken often depend more on the view of the social group to which one belongs than on the knowledge one possesses.

92 Part 2 Cooperation

- Moral viewpoints have a universal claim (scope). This can lead to closed mindedness and intolerance.
- Especially regarding moral points of view, the inner opponent is frequently absent.

Critical Questions

What do you think—are we approaching the limits of inner democracy? If, especially in moral issues, we are taking positions that originate from intuitions rather than from rational considerations, how then can you start to have a conversation with yourself about certain issues? And if our moral viewpoints have universal claims, what kind of conversation could we then have with each other? Inner democracy is, at its core, about the conversation you can have with yourself; or, formulated differently, it is a meta-dialogue between your different *I*-positions. Then there must be something to discuss: Oppositions, or learning from each other. If you adhere to moral values with universal claims, then there is not much to discuss. Or is there?

Exercise

First of all, go back to what you wrote under "From Your Own Experience," where you wrote down some of your opinions and ideas about a moral issue. Can you also indicate on what values you based that opinion? (Values such as justice, protection of privacy, equality of all people, etc.) Different opinions on certain moral issues can be based on different values. For example, when it comes to the question about how far intelligence services can look at our personal data, then the value of the protection of privacy stands diametrically opposed to the value of safety. This we call a moral dilemma: Two values stand in conflict with each other, and you have to weigh the pros and cons against each other. Moral dilemmas can also occur in your personal life. Suppose you know that a good friend has committed a serious misstep. Do you report this? Here we see the values of respect for justice and honesty on one side, in opposition to friendship and loyalty on the other.

You are now going to hold a discussion with yourself about a moral dilemma. Here are the steps to follow:

1. Describe a moral dilemma. This can be a social dilemma (from a current situation), a dilemma from the field of education, or a dilemma from your personal life. Describe the situation. The dilemma should be clear from your description of the situation. Formulate the *I*-positions that play a relevant role in this situation.
2. Identify the feelings and emotions that this dilemma evokes. What would you do on the basis of your emotions in this situation?

FIGURE 10.3 If you could decide, what would you say?
Source: Wikimedia Commons

3. Which values play a role in this situation, and how are you supposed to act on the basis of these values? What reasons can you give for your choice of behavior?
4. Now, start a discussion with other people, or with yourself, about how you should act in this situation. In this context, think about reasons and emotions. What choice are you making?
5. What role did reasons and emotions play in the making of your choice?

Reflecting

- The assumption in this chapter is that many of our moral views are inspired by emotions and gut responses. Do you recognize that in yourself?
- In Exercise 2, we described how you can start a conversation with yourself about moral dilemmas. Would you now use this method more often?
- If you think that this method is not very useful, how would you then start a conversation with yourself about moral issues? For developing inner democracy, it is important that you reflect on your personal way of dealing with moral problems and dilemmas.

Note

1. Black Pete is Saint Nicholas' little helper in Dutch tradition.

11

DEPOLARIZING OPPOSITION

Difference of opinion can be very useful: It can lead to other thoughts and new insights. However, people often grow apart, especially when they hold conflicting views, when the difference becomes unbridgeable, and when they become rebellious against each other. In society at large, we see that biased opinions and stereotyped images can dominate viewpoints toward other groups. How can we break through this? Or, formulated differently, How can we depolarize unbridgeable oppositions?

From Your Own Experience

Many people believe that we live in a polarized society. They think that there are many conflicting opinions, and that there are many opposing groups that cannot seem to come to a mutual understanding.

What do you think? Do you think that in society, many different groups exist that have opposing views? If you think so, can you name some of those groups, and can you also mention what some of the differences are between them? What opinions are being held by one group or by the other group? What, according to you, causes one group to be in opposition to another group, and causes them to be unable to come to an agreement?

Do you think you belong to a group that is aversive to another group? Which opinions does your group advocate, and which points of view are propagated by the other group? Why do you think these groups are in opposition to each other and can't reach a reconciliation?

Background Information

First of all, it is important to realize that life consists of opposites and contrasts. We cannot even comprehend the world without opposites. The world is full of them. We can only view something as beautiful if we also know what is ugly. We understand what darkness means when light has disappeared. We can only name something or someone tall if we know what it is to be small. We continuously use opposite pairs to make order of the world and understand it.

We also describe other people and ourselves in terms of opposites. We classify people as friendly or unfriendly, intelligent or stupid, open or closed, relaxed or anxious. It would be a misunderstanding to think we can fit everything in one category and therefore end up on just one side of the coin. Human beings are much more complex by nature. Opposites play a role in one and the same person because we may react very differently in different situations. At a party we are friendly and forthcoming, but we are earnest in a conversation with our physician. When we meet with friends we are open, but in contact with someone else, who wants to sell us a product, we may close ourselves off. If you want to take an initiative for something, you take the lead, but in a situation in which someone else is the leader, you take the position of follower. Depending on the situation, we find ourselves in different, even contrary, I-positions.

Can We Depolarize?

It gets really complicated if people hold points of view that are perceived as strongly opposed to each other. We saw in Chapter 10 that opinions that are morally laden are especially difficult to reconcile. Because moral opinions have a universal pretension (e.g. everybody should be thinking this way), this can lead to isolation and intolerance toward a vision that is viewed as opposed to the one we hold. When people disregard such a controversial view, they often consider the opinion of another person as "irrational," "crazy," "stupid," or even immoral and "inhumane." The result can be that people become opposed to each other in a fruitless way and become isolated from each other. Then we detect a continuous polarization. We can or will no longer bridge opposites, and the other person is no longer viewed as a conversation partner. Here we are confronted with an important question: How can we succeed in getting people to respect an opposing viewpoint, and are there circumstances in which people are willing to bridge opposing points of view? Is it possible to imagine yourself (vividly) in a situation to which you are normally opposed, a situation that could arise in which people come closer to each other and are willing to acknowledge the value of differing opinions?

FIGURE 11.1 How to solve a conflict?
Note that, as a consequence of virus containment measures in 2020, people are living together in a constrained environment in which social conflicts can easily emerge.
Source: Wikimedia Commons.

This idea was the starting point of researchers at the University of California (Tuller et al., 2015) who were interested in the circumstances in which people become depolarized. While they realized that in conflict situations it is very difficult to change established positions, they thought it was not impossible to do so. In this approach, they were inspired by a technique that is often applied in "empathy training" as part of relational therapy. In this therapy, someone who advocates a certain position is invited to place themselves in the position of another person who has a different point of view. The first person is then asked to describe, as accurately as possible, the view and also the feelings of their partner, a technique that is also labeled "paraphrasing." Then the other partner is asked to indicate if they felt understood by their partner. Often the result of this method is that the partner feels better understood than before. And also the speaker seems to be more competent to position themselves in the thoughts and feelings of the conversation partner. This method is used to break through "repetitive movements" by starting anew from previously held positions.

The researchers decided to apply this method to issues with a more political and moral component. Students were asked to read a text about a school policy that refused to hire teachers who were very overweight, and were asked to give their opinion about this policy. Did they agree with it or not? After giving their own opinion, the students were given a text that was supposedly written by their partner in the research design, but was in fact composed by the research team. From that text, a student could infer that their "partner" had an opinion about the issue that was completely different from their own. Then the participants in the experiments were asked to put themselves in the position of their partner. They were asked to describe, as best as they could, the opinion of their partner, using paraphrasing. In addition, the researchers told their subjects that their partner in this experiment would see this text, and that they would meet each other again. When, afterwards, all the participants in the experiment were asked again to give their opinion about the discriminatory school policy, it appeared that the opinions of the participants who had taken the position of their partner had, to some extent, moved in the direction of their partner's opinion.

The researchers went a step further. They repeated the experiment, but now the subjects in the research experiments were asked to give their opinions about abortion, an issue that has a heavier moral weight than the issue of admitting overweight teachers. They were told a story about a 16-year-old student who was raped by a friend of her mother. She discovered that she was 11 weeks pregnant, but did not want to keep the baby. The subjects in the experiment were asked the following question: What do you think about abortion in this case? This is a question that evokes a lot of emotions, among both proponents and opponents. However, the results were identical to the results in the overweight teachers experiment: The subjects who had paraphrased the position of the other partner moved more in the direction of their opponent than the subjects who had given just their own viewpoint.

The outcome of this research is important—abortion is a controversial issue in our society, with proponents and opponents who are vehemently opposed to each other and do not understand each other. We saw in Chapter 10 that there is a general inclination to hold onto a previously held moral point of view. The problem here was that previously held moral viewpoints could not easily be changed, or so it seemed. But this experiment shows that it is very possible, even around a moral issue, that people can depolarize. Two conditions should be mentioned in regard to this experiment. The people in the experiment are *accountable* for their own viewpoint—they are informed that their partner will get to see their written text. Also, there is a situation of *personal contact*—they were told that the subjects and their partners would meet again later. From this experiment, we can conclude that accountability and personal contact are important conditions for the depolarizing effect of paraphrasing.

The Other as Part of Ourselves

Through the method of paraphrasing, we force ourselves to step into the shoes of another person, which admittedly is not easy, especially when we find ourselves in a situation where the other person has completely different views. In a short period of time, we have to "step over" our own point of view that is so very precious to us. As we saw at the start of this chapter, it might help if we open up, more often than we normally do, the sharp or closed boundaries between ourselves and another person. This is especially important in a situation where people are inclined to withdraw themselves into the comfort zone of their own bubble and devalue, or even ignore, conflicting views. It is important that learning processes are stimulated that help us to cross the sharply demarcated boundaries between ourselves and the other. Crossing boundaries can be considered an important condition for the depolarization of rigidly closed positions.

The question is: How sharply demarcated are those boundaries and under what circumstances can they be crossed? Is the distinction between oneself and the other person actually as different as is often assumed? In this connection, it is interesting to look at some theories (Aron et al., 2005) claiming that the other person occupies a space not only outside ourselves, but *also* inside ourselves. The other who appears in your thoughts, memories, and visions of the future is a part of your own self. Other people can crawl inside your own world, solicited or unsolicited, and if that happens the other person can become a part of yourself and a welcome or unwelcome opponent in your daily thoughts. Moreover, when the other person is physically absent they can still enter your mind. If that happens often, your friend, girlfriend, father, mother, lover, or even an enemy, can become part of yourself. Sometimes it is not even very clear if a thought originates within yourself or was "originated" from somebody or something in the outside world.

Especially when you are in an intimate and trusted relationship with someone else, their perspective and even their identity can become, to a certain extent, part of yourself. We can find a nice illustration of this in the case of memory. It is a well-known phenomenon that people remember past successes as more recent, and past failures as further away in the past than they in fact were. Apparently, we allow pleasant memories to be closer in time than annoying ones. Aron et al. (2005) demonstrate that the same phenomenon occurs when people remember the successes and failures of their intimate partners. Their successes are experienced as more recent than their failures. This difference becomes less, or in fact disappears, when it concerns the memories of successes and failures of people who are more distanced from ourselves. In our memory, certain processes play a role that causes the memories about ourselves and other individuals to look more similar. This demonstrates that self and the other in our memory do not operate as if they are from completely different worlds, but are functioning in a rather overlapping way.

Bridging Oppositions between In-group and Out-group

We notice oppositions not just between persons, but also between groups in society. A well-known distinction in the social sciences is the difference between in-group and out-group. People derive their identity and self-esteem from the social group to which they belong (the in-group). At the same time, they feel inclined to put up boundaries against groups to which they think they do not belong (the out-group). And thus the members of the in-group ascribe qualities to themselves that they find absent from the out-group. The members of the in-group consider themselves as superior to those of the out-group. That is why we see an abundance of one-liners in the media that reflect prejudice and stereotyping regarding the out-group. In this context, think about people who consider themselves as part of a left-wing or right-wing political movement and who have different opinions about gender diversity, same-sex marriage, robot technology, climate change, immigration, race, ethnicity, etc.

In thinking about opposites there is often a master-term that is perceived as dominant, and a contrasting term that is considered subordinate (male–female, young–old, north–south, higher educated–lower educated). The contrasting pole of a dichotomy is often defined by negative terms, meaning that the positive characteristics of the master-term are absent.

Normally, people experience members of the in-group as part of themselves, but they do not consider members of the out-group this way. When the in-group is perceived as the dominant group, it functions as the master-term in relation to the out-group, which is considered to be subordinate. What would happen if you developed a friendship with someone from an out-group? This is a relevant question with regard to the boundaries between self and the other, because the distinction between in-groups and out-groups brings about sharp boundaries and oppositions, but friendship brings people closer to each other. Research shows that friendship with a member of the out-group not only brings the friend closer, but *also* the entire out-group (Aron, et al.; 2005). This means that emotional closeness with a member of the out-group can reduce the prejudices toward that group as a whole. We arrive here at the same conclusion we described earlier in this chapter when we discussed the technique of paraphrasing: Personal contact is an important lever if we want to break through the sharp boundaries between in-groups and out-groups and avoid extreme polarization. This happens when we place ourselves in the position of someone else who is starkly different from us. After all, friendship without prejudice is not contradictory. Friendship may exist without prejudice, and prejudice may exist without friendship. As long as you get stuck in one of these two possibilities, no change will take place. However, the simultaneity of friendship (no prejudice) and member of the out-group (yes, prejudice) leads us to a situation of contradiction that we want to avoid. Friendship then has an influence on a prejudice that you may have, with the possibility and resulting benefit that prejudices you hold towards an out-group can be corrected.

Opposition from within the In-group: Breaking through the Barriers

There is another way to break through the closed-off boundaries that demarcate a rigid point of view of the in-group: Asking advice of trusted experts. The credibility of an expert is very important—in general, people are inclined to disqualify an expert who is considered a member of a rival group. We do not seem to agree with experts when they belong to a group that is considered to be inferior. This problem caught the attention of Dan Kahan, who we met in Chapter 10 where we referred to his research on opinions about the risks of nanotechnology (Braman et al., 2007). There we saw that the large majority of the subjects in the research group knew nothing, or barely anything, about this technology, but still aired their opinions about it. They assumed a position not based on their knowledge, but influenced by the views of the ideological group to which they belonged. You probably remember that the people who held a more hierarchical point of view of society saw more advantages than disadvantages in this technology, while this was the other way around among more egalitarian-inclined individuals.

Because they were interested in the influence of the views of experts on the changing of previously held opinions, the researchers carried out a follow-up study (Braman et al., 2007; see also Mersch, 2016). They decided to give their research subjects the opinions of some fictitious experts. The expert from the hierarchical camp was illustrated by a picture of a formally dressed scientist wearing a tie, and book titles including *The Immigrant Invasion: Threatening the American Way of Life*, and *The War on American Manhood*. The expert from the

FIGURE 11.2 How to eliminate your enemies?
Source: Wikimedia Commons

egalitarian camp was wearing a crumpled shirt and a hipster beard. His expertise was illustrated by book titles such as *Three Social Evils: Sexism, Racism, and Homophobia*, and *Society as Family: One for All and All for One*. The expert from the egalitarian camp put forward arguments that the development of nano-technology should be delayed until more is known about the risks, an opinion that was often heard in the egalitarian camp. In contrast, the expert from the hierarchical camp defended his position in stating that this development of nanotechnology was worthwhile to be continued. The not-so-surprising results showed that the opinions of the research subjects polarized in different directions. Because they felt reassured by the experts in their original fixed opinion, they felt an extra confirmation in their existing opinion. The positions were directly opposed to each other: The in-group with their own experts, against the out-group also with their favorite experts. They were more firmly convinced about the correctness of their original opinions that were, after all, affirmed by an expert they trusted. The expert with a different opinion was simply not credible.

The research outcomes became really exciting when the researchers turned the tables. Contrary to expectations, the expert from the egalitarian camp assumed the position of advocate in favor of the further development of nanotechnology, while the expert from the hierarchical camp offered arguments against this technology. The surprising effect of this reversal was a depolarizing of the prior positions. Despite the fact that the arguments were in conflict with their prior opinions, the research subjects were now prepared to change their opinions. Apparently, the subjects were more open to arguments of an expert from their own camp who they thought was trustworthy. We need to notice here that the experiment made constructive use of invoking a contradiction that, apparently, changed the subjects' original position. This is comparable to a situation in which you get advice from a parent, grandparent, or friend you trust. The advice you are given, which is in conflict with the opinion you previously held, makes a huge impression because, after all, the person who is given this advice is very trustworthy.

At the conclusion of their study, the researchers added some advice on policy. They suggested it is advisable, where a new technology is introduced into society, to create a "deliberative climate" in which polarization would be reduced. In such a climate, the impression needs to be avoided that proponents of a new technology offer their expertise from an established political camp that one rejects. The researchers considered it more productive to create a "pluralistic environment" in which the public get to know the points of view from both pro and contra experts in each of the camps. When this process is applied to a sensitive and complex topic such as climate change, then it is not wise to let alarmists have a say from just the left, and sceptics from just the right, of the political spectrum. It is better to let both points of view be voiced from *inside* the left and *inside* the right camp. When the opinions are

102 Part 2 Cooperation

distributed this way, then the credibility of the experts would increase, and their influence on society would become stronger because there is now a disconnect between a political camp and the advice one gets. This creates a more open discussion climate in which different or contradictory opinions can be compared with each other.

Summarizing

- Opposites are part of our lives, just as there are contrary *I*-positions in ourselves.
- Opposing views can lead to unfruitful polarization if they are associated with rigid or fixed boundaries between in-groups and out-groups.
- Depolarizing can be advanced via learning, paraphrasing, and personal contact with other individuals who hold opposing points of view.
- Depolarizing can also be stimulated by experts we trust.
- Experts can only stimulate depolarization if they present a contradictory point of view that derives from one's own ideological group.

Critical Questions

In the text we have seen that opposites are important in dealing with issues in life, and trying to understand various puzzling phenomena. What do you think? Is this a rather simplistic starting point, because between black and white we find very many gray shades, and between pro and con we find many nuances?

In the text we have described how previously held conflicting opinions can be changed, a finding that is supported by research. Do you think this is demonstrated convincingly, maybe because you recognize this in yourself and in other people? Or do you think this is not the case? Can you give some reasons for your point of view about this issue?

Preparation of the Exercise

We have already done the exercises about the functions of summarizing and paraphrasing. In a simpler way, we described this in Chapter 4 when we explained the three-step model. In Chapter 9 we concentrated on listening and summarizing as the core of the practice. In the present chapter, two points should be emphasized:

- in a conversation, you summarize the statements in the same words as your partner has used in the conversation;
- paraphrasing is what you do in a question-form: Do I understand you correctly when I summarize it as follows? ...

The challenge is to listen very carefully to what the other person is saying. Paraphrasing is considered a form of interpreting, and you need to check if your interpretation is accurate.

From the research of Tuller et al. (2015) we noticed that summarizing is not sufficient and paraphrasing is necessary.

Excercise

You can practice paraphrasing in two ways.

2.1 Choose an article from a newspaper that reflects an opinion you totally disagree with. National newspapers always have daily opinion pieces. You can easily find such statements on their websites. The most useful piece in this context is a piece written by someone you do not like.

Write a summary (100 to 200 words) in which you convincingly describe, in your own words, the opinions and arguments of the author of the opinion piece. Afterwards, check with someone else if your description came close to the arguments of the author.

2.2 Start a discussion in a small group about a complex topic, preferably one with a heavy moral component. Below we offer some suggestions for topics, but you can of course choose a subject from contemporary news stories. Stay with the procedure outlined below.

Assign a moderator who invites each person to speak, and eventually leads the discussion in order to prevent the conversation coming to a premature end.

- The first person says: "I think that ... , because ... "
- The next person responds by paraphrasing what their predecessor said, and then gives their own input: "[Name] thinks ... , because ... ; I agree (or disagree) with that, because ... "

This exercise forces you to listen very attentively to each other and to place yourself in someone else's position. Only afterwards can you give your remarks about what other people have said in the conversation.

Some examples of questions that can lead to firmly expressed statements are:

- Should everyone who lives in a certain country have the same rights?
- Should schools and teachers be held responsible for each child achieving the highest possible education level?
- Is a happy life something you have to strive for yourself, or is it more a matter of "pure luck"?

104   Part 2 Cooperation

- Should we close the country to people from other countries in a case of pandemic?
- Should we, in our country, promote a social points system like in China, in which people receive points for good behavior (e.g., informal care-giving, voluntary work) and then get rewarded with access to care facilities (e.g., in health care, or education)?

Reflecting

- In "From Your Own Experience," you described a group you belong to and another group that is alien to you. How could you depolarize this opposition? Have the study of the text and the exercises changed your opinions about this subject?
- From the research we described in this chapter, it seems that the function of personal contact is of great importance. No personal contact exists with people you know only via media or electronic devices. Every day you see and hear, via media, negative opinions about people you dislike. How much respect can you have for the opinions of those people? What did you learn from the exercises in this chapter?

12

FROM DEBATE TO DIALOGUE

When elections occur, we see politicians in debate with one another. There is an election contest for your vote as well as for the votes of other people. Politicians want to win elections, and therefore a debates takes place so we, as voters, know the differences between their points of view. However, there is an important distinction between a debate and a dialogue. In contrast to a debate, one cannot *win* a dialogue, and it does not allow you to simply be pro or con a certain issue. A dialogue is all about learning from each other. In this chapter we describe and differentiate the characteristics of debate and dialogue, and especially the various possibilities for understanding inner democracy.

From Your Own Experience

We all have conversations with each other. In the workplace, in organizations, at home, with family members, and also in school, we sometimes have conversations that we call dialogues. When do you think a conversation is a dialogue? What are the characteristics of a a dialogue? Can you describe them?

Background Information

In the public domain, we are familiar with following debates on various media. On TV, we see participants furiously voice a certain position. In newspapers, we see journalists and readers give their opinions, which are often disputed by other readers. On radio programs, listeners can express their opinions for or against a particular point of view, with few nuances for alternative possibilities. On Twitter and Facebook, people dispute with each other about the "right" viewpoint. In contrast, we hear and see less from people who are engaged in a dialogue, who listen carefully to each other and who develop their points of view in conjunction with each other. Apparently, this is less "exciting" and, as a viewer or listener, it is harder to make sense of the different opinions and viewpoints precisely because the exchanges take place in a dialogue mode.

Debate and dialogue are completely different ways to communicate with each other about a certain topic, and each requires a very different approach. A question we can ask is: "What are the most important differences and what are the goals you want to reach?" At the end of this chapter we will give an overview of the most important differences between debate and dialogue. But first we will turn to their specific characteristics.

Debate and Dialogue: Different Ways to Communicate

In a debate, a participant holds a certain position that can be disputed by another person with an opposing point of view. The purpose is to defend or oppose a certain standpoint, and each position has its proponents and opponents. In public debates, the participants dispute each other within a certain time frame, with fixed schedules for each speaker. Often there is a third party present who is supposed to hold an independent position and who organizes the debate. Sometimes a public jury is present that decides who has won the debate, and there are responses from listeners or viewers who evaluate the debate from their own points of view. We see well-known examples of specific debates in election periods, when the candidates are running for president or for the House of Representatives.

FIGURE 12.1 Debate
Source: Wikimedia commons

A debate can be more or less formalized. We see this in a legal context, where we see a prosecuting attorney who accuses the defendant and a defending attorney who defends the person who is accused. But debates can also take place in informal settings. This occurs when someone gives their opinion and receives a reply from someone else. Then the first speaker repeats their original point of view or comes up with more arguments to bolster their original position. Characteristic of a debate is that the original point of view of the debater does not really change, but might even get stronger during the exchange of arguments. After all, each move of the other party calls for new arguments designed to strengthen the original position of the speaker.

Dialogue is a completely different form of communication. It is a non-polarizing way of exchanging ideas and experiences, and is focused not on opposition but on cooperation. The goal is not to let *one* vision prevail above the other, but to reach a more comprehensive perspective in which multiple points of view and experiences come to expression and are integrated. A certain communication formula can be considered a dialogue when the participants respect not only the arguments of the other person, but also their stories, experiences, and feelings. The issue here is not just to listen to what is said by the other person, but to also understand what is not explicitly expressed, in other words, to what the speaker *intends to convey*. This requires "high-quality listening" as we discussed in Chapter 9. Listening, certainly *good* listening, is not an easy thing to do. When another person is speaking, we are often inwardly preparing for what we are going to say in response to their claims or viewpoints. In short, we often pay more attention to our own views instead of those of our partner in the conversation.

FIGURE 12.2 Dialogue (replaced by electronic communication in corona-time)
Source: Wikimedia Commons

108 Part 2 Cooperation

By opening yourself up to another person and by using the technique of high-quality listening, a greater openness arises towards the views and opinions of the other person compared to a debate situation. Thanks to this openness, we are able to change our original opinions, viewpoints, or experiences because of something that has been said or expressed by our dialogue partner. This requires a flexible change in perspective, as we have described in Chapter 4. There we discussed the three-step model as a foundation for dialogue. Here we refer briefly to this model and expand on it a little more.

- Step 1: Describe your experience, story, feeling, or insight to another person.
- Step 2: The other person listens and responds to your verbal and non-verbal expressions, and tries to figure out the meaning underlying these expressions.
- Step 3: You return to your original view, story, feeling, or insight in step 1 and develop it further by including elements of your conversation partner's response in step 2.

In this model, step 3 is the greatest challenge in a dialogical situation. If one succeeds in taking this step, two things can occur that do not happen in a debate. First, the participants' viewpoints will move more closely towards each other because they incorporate elements of the other person's views and thereby allocate space to those views in their own position. As a result, something *communal* occurs in which the participants have the feeling that they share an idea, insight, or experience with each another. Furthermore, step 3 involves that *something new* happens between and inside the participants that was not present before. They can reach an *Aha-Erlebnis*[1] that expresses the pleasure of a new insight or discovery. In the dialogue mode, step 3 adds something new that "rises up" between or among the participants and that they can share with each other. That is why the result of a dialogue is hard to predict compared to a debate. In a productive dialogue, new venues are explored by the participants together.

Why is Dialogue Sometimes Difficult?

As described, dialogue sounds beautiful and easy, but making it work is difficult for participants and for some even impossible. Why is it so difficult? In an extensive analysis of the differences between debate and dialogue, American educationalists Hyde & Bineham (2000) claim that dialogue is often not possible because people cherish and defend their identity, which may work as a barrier that might prevent a real dialogue. We all display personal identity (I as fighting for justice), gender identity (I as hetero, homosexual, lesbian, transgender), national identity (I as a citizen of my own country), religious identity (I as a Catholic, I as a Muslim), or cultural identity (I as coming from Africa). People are attached to a certain identity because it shows where they stand in the world, what and where they belong to, and where they come from. Above all, a feeling of identity gives people a sense of self-esteem: The values of the group you belong to reflects the values you believe yourself to have. To engage in a dialogue can be threatening when in a conversation the participants bring something to the forefront that might be experienced as undermining your identity and associated with your feeling of self-esteem. It is then difficult to step in the shoes of another person and empathize with them, and to let the views of another person affect you and influence your own thoughts and feelings.

A problem arises if everyone wants to hold on firmly to their own identity and is not willing or able to look over its boundaries. After all, the world would then be fragmented in a conglomeration of people who demarcate their own identity and turn defensive as soon as they are confronted by people who take a different stance. If everyone closes themselves off in their own identity bubble, then no communication beyond the boundaries of one's self would be possible. That is why dialogue is so important, because it offers the opportunity to go beyond those boundaries. Dialogue is essential in a globalizing and boundary-crossing society (Friedman, 1999).

Another reason why dialogue is so complex is the situational conditions in which a dialogue takes place. It is a well-known phenomenon that people do not immediately open themselves up to strangers they have not met before, and who are different or do not conform to the norms we are used to (Ma-Kellams & Blascovich, 2012). Openness is essential to start a dialogue, as we have seen previously in this chapter. Furthermore, dialogue is dependent on the *atmosphere* of a conversation (Hermans & Hermans-Konopka, 2010). No dialogue will succeed in an atmosphere that is too formal, tense, or hostile. Dialogue can only arise in a sphere of mutual trust and safety—as we can observe in a classroom environment. Only then are people willing and able to open themselves up to other people and listen to each other's opinions and experiences.

A dialogue's degree of difficulty also depends on the extent to which the participants agree or disagree with each other. Disagreement is important, because we learn more from each other when our views are different than when we apparently seem to think and act the same way. If we agree fast and furiously with one another, that might be efficient in situations in which we have to make rapid decisions, but then we do not learn much from each other. However, disagreeing with one another is more difficult than agreeing with one another, because it can be painful when your own opinion doesn't receive the appreciation that you may need to give a boost to your self-esteem.

How can Dialogue be Stimulated?

In their recommendations for stimulating dialogue, Hyde & Bineham (2000) refer to an old ritual used by Native Americans in their councils. In a classroom situation, teachers can invite students to sit in a circle and to start a dialogue about a topic that invokes different questions. Then they each get the opportunity to express their opinions. The person who is talking holds an attractively decorated "talking stick" in their hand.[2] As long as this person is talking, no-one may interrupt them. The people in the group are asked to listen carefully until the speaker has made their point. Only after that is the stick passed along to the next speaker. This ritual has variants. One variant is that when the speaker is finished, they then can choose someone who should repeat what has just been said in their own words. Only when the speaker feels that they are well understood will the stick be passed along.

The benefit of this method is that it prevents the discussion from getting bogged down in a confusing battle of words and numerous fragmented viewpoints. Participants who often dominate a conversation are now forced to listen, while participants stay quiet who most of the time will get the chance to speak and hold the attention of the other participants. Using this method, we discern many diverse *I*-positions without a dominating position that might otherwise suppress other positions. This method also has the advantage that the speaker feels accepted and safe, and therefore an atmosphere of trust can arise in the group. By talking and listening in a safe atmosphere, students can show their insecurities and explore their inner gray areas. This is in contrast to the black-and-white thinking and reasoning that often characterizes a debate.

A "circle-conversation" allows participants to look at all other participants in the dialogue. Some participants might prefer an open circle, without tables or other objects between the participants. A table can function as a line of defense. Openness of space can facilitate contact with other participants, which is essential

FIGURE 12.3 Talking stick
Source: Wikimedia commons

for a dialogue. This can be expressed verbally by asking questions, and non-verbally by our body posture and facial expression.

To facilitate a dialogue it is also necessary that we ask the "right" questions, preferably open questions that can lead to multiple answers. Fundamental questions, that have a wide scope and that can deepen the dialogue, are to be preferred over specific and detail-oriented questions, which often have hardly any relevance for the participants. A dialogue can also become inhibited when the group is too large. An optimal group for a dialogue exercise has six to eight participants. This range is optimal because the participants will feel secure to freely express themselves, and that they are in a trusting atmosphere.

Dialogue will also be fostered by choosing a common theme or goal. It is desirable that the participants endorse the importance of a particular goal or topic. It is very helpful when the participants in a group dialogue share at least *some* values about a certain topic or issue. In general, when there is sufficient commonality, then there is a realistic chance that the participants will pay attention to other viewpoints and opinions. When people differ from each other in *all* aspects, a dialogue would be impossible because the participants would remain strangers toward each other. Only when there exists a common underlying base can people acknowledge their differences and respond to them. A certain level of commonality is a prerequisite for responding to differences and alternative points of view between participants.

From Debate to Dialogue

The above discussion does not imply that dialogue is better than debate in all aspects, and we do not mean to propose that debate should be replaced by dialogue in all circumstances. Depending on the situation and motives of the participants, either a debate or a dialogue may be preferred as a mode of conversation. A debate has the advantage that the participants can express and articulate their own position regarding a certain issue and share it with the audience. Their opinions can then be tested on their validity and on the persuasiveness of the underlying ideas. The logic behind the arguments and the credibility of the positions presented can be brought to the surface. Debate shows what someone's position is and makes it possible to get an impression of someone's knowledge and expertise. And via high-quality listening we can gain more knowledge about a particular subject.

While debate is focused on presenting and defending one's own position, the power of dialogue lies in the common exploration of existing positions and exploration of new ones. It is a quest for the unknown experiential world of the other, precisely in their "being different." The dialogue acknowledges the other as "another I," an "alter ego," who is different from me but also "like me." This ambiguity makes the dialogue an exploration of a domain of the other, and even of oneself, that is partly unknown—but an area that becomes familiar via this quest. In addition, dialogue is a form of communication that can bring people together and can create something communal that wasn't there before.

To understand the concepts of dialogue and debate, it is very important that we understand they are two very different forms of communication. A debate is comparable to a boxing match with a winner and a loser. The parties are standing opposed to each other, and duel with each other based on the strength of their arguments. The result is that one person comes out as stronger than the other. Dialogue looks more like a tango in which the parties are closely connected and move together in various directions, as we summarize in Table 12.1.

Finally, we need to be very careful when using these concepts. The term "dialogue" is used frequently in the media, with the result that the exceptional quality of this form of communication fades away and can no longer be distinguished from general "chattering with each other." Especially in political forums and discussions, the term "dialogue" often hides differences in power and conflicts of interests. The columnist Jan Kuitenbrouwer (2014) has it right when he says that the term "dialogue" is often used as a "euphemism for the polite exchange of unshakable points of view."

Summarizing

- Debate and dialogue are very different forms of communication, each having its own characteristics.
- Dialogue is difficult—it can be prevented by people who want to protect their own identity.
- Dialogue can be stimulated by procedures that give each participant space to express and share their own opinion.
- Dialogue and debate do not preclude one another, but can supplement each other.

TABLE 12.1 Differences between debate and dialogue

Debate	*Dialogue*
The only right solution	Alternative solutions
Positions are closed and are predictable	Positions are flexible and new positions may emerge
Changing of position or stance is considered a defeat	Changing of opinion is part of a learning process
High degree of certainty	Tolerance for uncertainty and ambiguity
Positions stand in opposition to each other	A dialogical space arises *among* different positions

From Debate to Dialogue **113**

Critical Questions

In the text we noted that great importance is given to the value of dialogue: Learning from each other. Can you learn something from any individual you come to meet, and so can you engage in a dialogue with everyone? Or is it better to search for a good conversation partner?

And what about inner dialogue? Can you have a coherent dialogue with yourself?

Does that happen in the same way as a dialogue with another person, as we described in this chapter?

Exercise

Participating in a dialogue is easier said than done. Your identity is at stake, you need to listen very well and carefully, and then also deliver your contribution to a common project. A dialogue can have several forms. The communication form described below (from Kessels, Boers & Mostert, 2002) is very easily applied and doesn't need much preparation.

The best way to conduct this dialogue is with six to eight participants. Assign one of the participants as a group leader. You can use the "talking stick" method.

Follow these seven steps:

Time
Discuss with each other how much time you want to spend on a certain subject. With six people you can have a good dialogue in 30 minutes.

Topic
Decide on the topic of the conversation. Let one of the group participants take notes on important aspects of the topic. It will work well when someone writes a few simple words on a board.

Questions
Give everyone the opportunity to ask questions about the topic. These are questions that can be analyzed further.

Experiences
Everyone who wants to can describe their own experiences in relation to the subject. This may involve concrete examples about how you experience the specific topic in your private life, work situation, or educational environment.

Reponses
Other people may respond to the experiences that are brought forward via questions, remarks, and reflections. This is the phase in which you need to be

114 Part 2 Cooperation

very attentive so that the atmosphere of a dialogue is preserved—meaning thinking aloud with each other, instead of arguing with each other.

Essence

Once the most important experiences and questions have been discussed, the group leader asks all the participants what was the essence of the topic for them. What does it mean to you? To what should we pay the most attention? Then everyone should express in a few short sentences what is important for them, and share it with the others in the group. If you like, you can write this down.

Discussing afterwards

Take some time to reflect on the discussion. Was it really a dialogue? Did you contribute to the dialogue, or to a dialogical atmosphere? Next time, what should we pay more attention to?

Reflecting

- Exercise 2 involves a dialogue in a small group. A good dialogue with more people will take up much more time. We don't always spend so much time—or do we … ?
- Dialogue is more like an attitude. Do you agree with that? How would you describe that attitude? And do you have that attitude, or have you achieved it now?
- Look back at what you described as characteristics of a dialogue under the heading "From Your Own Experience." Are there similarities with what you think now, and have you learned something new?

Notes

1. The German noun *Erlebnis* refers to an experience or event that affects or involves a person (Cambridge Dictionary).
2. For the origin and meaning of the stick, see First People, American Indian Legends, Talking Stick: https://www.firstpeople.us/FP-Html-Legends/TraditionalTalkingStick-Unknown.html.

13

EMPATHY

A Frequently Used Word, but Difficult to Express

Empathy is an important element in a democratic society. It appears in various forms. And empathy also plays a significant role in our inner self. Do you think you are empathic? In this chapter, you have a chance to check this out.

From Your Own Experience

With whom do you feel or experience empathy? Can you briefly describe the person and what you feel exactly? Are there also people with whom you feel no, or hardly any, empathy? Do you have an explanation for this difference? What according to you, is empathy? Write it down.

Background Information

Every human being has the tendency to observe other people from an "I" point of view. You observe your environment and other people from a certain perspective. You are here, and they are there. It is not possible to detach oneself completely from the position you occupy: I as a man or woman, child or adult, student or teacher, young or old. We are in a natural way bound to a position in time and space, which entails that we observe people and objects around us from that specific perspective. In a certain way we all are egocentric because we cannot help but look at the world around us from the positions we ourselves occupy.

However, we can also imagine the position of another person and perceive the world from their perspectives. To take the perspective of another person, and to observe and experience the world from their point of view, is what is usually understood by "empathy." Developmental psychologists such as Roth-Hanania and colleagues (2000) have reported that the first signs of empathy are already

116 Part 2 Cooperation

present in infants. They do not cry just when they are hungry or thirsty, but also when they hear another baby cry. These researchers also showed that 12–18-month-old infants imitate the facial expressions of other people, and 18–24-month-old infants may already start to help another person in distress.[1] Only when they are capable of mastering a language, are they able to express verbally that they feel what is going on in another person. We are talking here about emotional empathy, which is apparently already present very early in life. This is different from cognitive empathy, which develops later.

"Theory of Mind" as Cognitive Empathy

In the literature, empathy is often associated with the development of what psychologists have described as a "theory of mind," which refers to the ability to assess another person's point of view and at the same time to notice the differences between one's own perspective and the perspective of another individual. The box below describes how researchers decided if children had developed a theory of mind.

THEORY OF MIND

In a well-known research project described by the developmental psychologists Carlson & Moses (2001), two children, Bert and Ernie, play with a ball. After a little while, Bert puts the ball in a blue box and leaves the room. Ernie takes the ball from the blue box and plays with it for a little while. Then he puts the ball in a red box and leaves the room. After a little while Bert comes back and wants to play with the ball. At that moment, children who have watched this scenario are asked: "Where do you think the ball is according to Bert?," followed by the question: "Where is the ball really?" Children who have developed a "theory of mind" will say that Bert thinks the ball is in the blue box, while in reality the ball is in the red box. Children who have not yet mastered a theory of mind expect that Bert is searching for the ball in the red box. This shows that they are not yet able to assume the perspective of another individual.

The research demonstrates that a theory of mind requires that we can distinguish between our own perspective and that of another person. We have to be able to go beyond our own perspective to assume the perspective of another person, and, above all, give priority to the perspective of the other individual. Apparently, children around 3 years of age are bound to their own perspective and have not yet developed the capacity to perceive the same situation from the perspective of another person. If a toy looks a certain way from the front, it's hard to imagine that it might look different to another child from a different perspective. Once children reach the age of 4–5 years, they have mastered the capacity to look at an object from different perspectives.

To assume the position of someone else is not self-evident. It requires effort, because we are naturally inclined to view things from our own perspective. To reach insight into this phenomenon, Gerstadt, Hong & Diamond (1994) made use of a different method. They showed 3–7-year-old children one picture that displayed the sun, and another picture that depicted the moon and stars. They asked the children a difficult question, namely to say "night" when they saw a white picture with a yellow sun, and to say "day" when they were shown a dark picture with a moon and stars. The research team assumed that children who were able to give this inverse response could control their spontaneous impulse—sun belongs to day, and moon and stars belong to night. Thereafter, they showed a correlation between the results of the "theory of mind" tests and those of the picture test. It seemed that children who were able to take the perspective of another child in the situation of the two boxes and the ball, were more capable of controlling their spontaneous impulses to the day–night instruction than the children who had not yet developed a theory of mind. From this research, we can conclude that assuming the perspective of another individual requires at least that one should put one's own direct impulse on a back burner, at least for a little while. And, as this research shows, this requires some effort. It also demonstrates

FIGURE 13.1 How can you cultivate compassion in your life?
Source: Wikimedia Commons

118 Part 2 Cooperation

that our relationship with others is connected with the way we deal with our own impulses.

Three Forms of Empathy

Research into the theory of mind has certainly been instrumental for understanding empathy. However, it is not sufficient to do justice to the versatility of this capability. The most important constraint is that theory of mind is, above all, cognitive in nature and pays little attention to the emotions of another person. This problem was addressed by two famous psychologists, Daniel Goleman, expert in the field of emotional intelligence, and Paul Ekman, who has done extensive research into emotional facial expressions (see Goleman, 2007). They offered a definition of empathy that was wider than just the capacity to place oneself cognitively in another's position. They distinguished three forms of empathy: Cognitive empathy, emotional empathy, and compassion. In what follows we take a closer look at these three variations of empathy.

Cognitive empathy

The first form, cognitive empathy, is the capacity to understand what another person is experiencing from within their frame of reference. Sometimes this is called "perspective taking." There is a problem with this definition. The emphasis here is to place oneself in the *position* that someone else occupies from their own perspective, but not in how another person *emotionally experiences* a particular position. Some people are very able to assume the perspective of another person, but use this capacity purely for their own interest and benefit. One can think in this respect of swindlers who are very skilled in estimating what is going on in the inner lives of their victims and what they think is important, and then use this understanding for deception and fraudulence. People with a narcissistic personality disorder serve as another example. Individuals like these are often adept at placing themselves cognitively in the position of another, and use this capacity to manipulate and exploit them. With charm and deception, they often succeed in manipulating others to benefit their own self-grandiosity. One can also refer to the behavior of "Machiavellians" who, with complete disregard for any moral issues, try to exercise control over other people, just to benefit themselves. We notice a similar problem with people who are often described as "psychopaths." They lack compassion, do not experience guilty feelings when they behave in an anti-social way, and go after their goals without any moral compass or concern for other people. These examples indicate that there are people who can effectively place themselves cognitively in the position of another person. However, they lack the compassion that is needed to take the feelings of other people into account and respond to those feelings with emotional empathy.[2]

Empathy **119**

Emotional empathy

For Goleman and Ekman, these findings were the reasons to distinguish another category, emotional empathy. This plays an important role in relations where people feel involved with each other and in which they "tune into" the feelings of another person. This is, for instance, a necessary component in parent–child relationships, in friendships, and in the contact between teacher and student. In short, it is essential in contexts where it is necessary to take account of the feelings of others and to respect them. But this aspect of empathy also has its limitations. In some situations, people can experience an excess of emotional empathy, and they feel as if they are losing themselves in the emotions of another individual, and are unable to maintain a sufficient distance from the other person's emotional baggage. Exactly in situations in which one is trying to support another individual, it is often necessary to place oneself in the position of the other individual, *but* also to preserve a distance in order to avoid becoming overwhelmed by the other person's emotions.

Compassion

Precisely because emotional empathy can be associated with a lack of emotional distance, researchers have distinguished a third form of empathy, which they call compassion. This form of empathy is necessary not only to share in the emotions of another person, but also as a motive to offer support and help to the other individual. Clients who look for help, or students who ask their teachers for help for personal reasons, expect more than just a willing ear. They expect that the teacher or social worker is willing and prepared to act to improve a situation on behalf of the student or client. Of course, for a teacher it is easier to help a student in whom they recognize themself, than to help a student with a vastly different experiential outlook on the world. This requires teachers to have a very broad capability to empathize with their students, who will have different experiences and will vary in their outlooks on the world.

Compassion encompasses emotional empathy, but includes an additional active component. We should not just resonate with a sympathetic feeling as a sounding board, but also keep a certain distance, in order to act in an effective way. In other words, compassion requires more than just emotional empathy. One should adopt a meta-position, a concept that we discussed in Chapter 5. There we described how by assuming a meta-position, we can take a certain distance and oversee several *I*-positions of the other and ourselves, link them together, and correlate them with our actions and behavior. In the case of compassion, you can transpose yourself into the emotions of another person, but you can also look at the broader surroundings of this particular person and the various positions they occupy. This means that a teacher, when approached by a student, pays attention not just to the emotions and feelings of the student, but also to their position

120 Part 2 Cooperation

within their family, and their relations with fellow students. The teacher also pays attention to their own *I*-positions, which are invoked by the student. The teacher wants to help the student, but they should also be aware of their position in relation to other students, and as a member of the teaching team that also deals with this particular student. The advantage of this meta-position is that you can become aware of your own *I*-positions and those of other people. This way, the teacher will notice where the various *I*-positions complement each other, and what their limitations are. The meta-position is necessary to prevent you from becoming completely overwhelmed by the emotions of another person, and it might help you to get involved with the other person from a wider perspective. In a situation where a student is overwhelmed by certain emotions, the teacher can invite them to take up a meta-position to gain a better insight into the situation. A well-developed meta-position will help people to develop feelings and insights into the relations between the various *I*-positions in themselves and in other people. Tensions and conflicts that might arise among different and contradictory *I*-positions can be dealt with more easily if you strengthen your empathic skills.

Empathy and Education

In the field of education, we notice a strong interest in the importance of empathy in the development of younger pupils. The couple Norma and Seymour Feshbach, both psychologists who practiced for years in the field of education and pedagogy, have shown that empathy can be not only studied, but also stimulated. In their literature review (Feshbach & Feshbach, 2009) they indicate that, for young people as well as adults, it is possible to strengthen empathic capability with exercises and training. If one succeeds in showing people that they resemble each other in similar experiences more than they think, and when they share these experiences, then their capacity to empathize with other individuals will become strengthened. Role-playing is a useful method in this regard. To feel sympathy for a real-life person, or a character in a fictional novel, or a historical person, is a method in role-playing that is often used to promote empathy. Also important is the content of narratives invoked by role-playing. It appears that people feel empathy especially with people in situations that show failure, misfortune, or a casualty. The painfully dramatic aspects of a person's life generate more feelings of empathy than their successes and triumphs. Comparisons with other people who do better than you often invoke feelings of envy, but comparisons with people who do worse than you often invoke more empathic feelings.

Also, musical practice can be used as a method to stimulate empathic responses. Feshbach and Feshbach mention research showing that musical activities such as singing together, playing instruments, or listening to music together increase levels of empathy and social behavior. Writing and drawing are also methods used to foster empathy (Lengelle, 2016). Group processes that arise when people try to solve problems together are also useful to stimulate empathy. Where learning processes do not just occur in an individual situation, but are shared by members of a group who have the same goals, students are more dependent on each other and thus a more direct exchange of thoughts and feelings can occur.

Empathy is also important in creating a democratic attitude. Feshbach and Feshbach refer to literature showing that stimulating empathy influences the reduction of prejudices towards other ethnic groups. Empathic people can place themselves within the perspectives and feelings of people who are members of a group to which they do not belong. This can lead to less prejudice, less conflict, and more social openness than where empathy is absent.

Empathy and Inner Democracy

What is the connection between empathy and inner democracy? The answer can be found in the special nature of *I*-positions as described in Chapter 1. There we explained how the concept of "*I*-position" makes it possible to assume the perspective of another person as an extension of our own self. Another person can then function as an *I*-position in our own mind. In this way we become connected to our parents and teachers, friends, and colleagues, so that they come to take up space in our inner selves. Sometimes you can even experience the feeling of *being* someone else. Then you notice: Now I talk like my father, or my sister,

FIGURE 13.2 Empathy requires eye contact and listening in an open way
Source: Wikimedia Commons

122 Part 2 Cooperation

brother, friend. Also in Chapter 1 we described how, for the formation of your identity, it is necessary to make a *distinction* between your own *I*-position and the *I*-position that someone else takes up in your own self. It may be that someone else, maybe a parent, can be so dominant in the organization of your inner life that you do not know if wishing something is what you yourself really want, or what the mother or father in yourself wants.

Another person can play a role as another *I*-position in yourself. The question is: How far do you want to go with empathy? Do you only express empathy with someone who is very similar to you, or can you have empathy with somebody who is very different from you? Or can you even have empathy with a person who is your opponent? This is a question that cannot easily be answered. The answer could be an indication of empathy with limited scope (I only feel empathy toward people who are close to me), or empathy with wider scope (I can also feel empathy with people who are very different from me). We detect more inner democracy in the second example than in the first. After all, you are able to include other individuals in yourself, even when they are different from yourself. Stronger still, you are capable of showing a certain compassion toward them.

Summarizing

- Developing a theory of mind is important for placing oneself in the position of another person.
- We differentiate between three forms of empathy: Cognitive empathy, emotional empathy, and compassion. The third form also includes an active component.
- Empathy can be strengthened by education and through role-playing, drawing techniques, music, and other artistic activities.
- Inner democracy requires giving space to the other in yourself, even if the other person is your opponent.

Critical Questions

In this chapter we presented empathy as a satisfying quality that we all should develop. But the question is: Is this advisable for everybody in all situations? In Part 1 we warned about "too soft an attitude" regarding openness to another person. In this chapter, we have also suggested that we can sometimes be too empathetic. What do you think? Do you sometimes display too much empathy towards another person? Can you then handle that degree of empathy, can you regulate it with an on-or-off button? Is that possible? And if so, would you make use of such a button? And when?

Empathy 123

Exercises

Exercise 1

Emotional empathy

"Place yourself in the shoes of another person. There are always people who do not immediately invoke your sympathy: A teacher, somebody on the street where you live, the manager of the company where you work. You occasionally meet people, or watch them on TV, who provoke negative feelings in you. Can you think about somebody like that? What made you choose this specific individual? Now imagine that you see this person in a completely different environment, such as at home on a Saturday afternoon playing with their children, a situation in which this individual is in a completely different position and shows certain sides of themself of which you were not aware. Just let your imagination do the work. What are the characteristics you ascribe to the person in that new situation? How can you reconcile this with your prejudices? Does this exercise increase your emotional empathy?"

Exercise 2

Cognitive empathy

Place yourself in the position of another person. In several previous chapters we have described how to place yourself in the perspective of another person (Chapters 4, 9, and 11 in particular). This is meant not just in a figurative sense, but also in a literal sense: Other people often see many other things differently from you, even while looking at the same object or events. The American animal psychologist Alexandra Horowitz (2013) knows from her own experience that while taking walks with her dog, animals react to visual cues differently from human beings. She applied that result to humans: She took a walk with 11 different people, an architect, a toddler, an artist, etc., and asked them what they observed. All these people noticed different things and gave different impressions about what they saw on the same walking route.

> The book that describes the result of this experiment is an enlargement of an experience with which we all are familiar. We all have sometimes experienced the same object or event, but have a slightly different narrative to describe it. Try this with someone whose background is very different from yours. You can also use a video or picture for illustration purposes.

Reflecting

- Exercises 2 and 3 are examples that demonstrate that you can do these exercises over and over. The capability to develop empathy occurs only when you practice it frequently. With whom do you feel no empathy at all?

124   Part 2 Cooperation

In which person can you not really place yourself? Can you train yourself to look at the world from their perspective and to empathize with them? What would be the advantage, for you and for the other?

- Finally, go back to your initial view on empathy that you expressed in "From Your Own Experience" at the start of this chapter? Describe what has changed from your original point of view? What did you learn?

Notes

1. Recent research has shown that, as early as their second year, children can demonstrate altruistic behavior when they notice that another person is in need of food. In a study of 19-month-old children, developmental researchers Barragan, Brooks & Meltzoff (2020) found that, even when hungry, children gave a tasty snack, that had been given to them, to a stranger in need.
2. Empathy has received much attention in the psychological science literature. For an overview of neurological studies, see Decety & Jackson (2004). Psychotherapeutic aspects are mentioned by Elliot et al. (2011).

EPILOGUE TO PART 2

Democracy cannot function without opposition, nor can inner democracy. This is what we have described in Part 1 of this book: Opposition, especially within yourself, is a movement from one *I*-position to an opposing one. And, just as in a democracy at large, we see the same processes occurring in inner democracy: After opposition, we look for cooperation and solutions, and how to bridge those different viewpoints and opinions so that we can learn from them.

But this is easier said than done. Especially when values are at stake, when our opinions are morally charged, we find it difficult to view our initial opinion from a different perspective. It is difficult to acknowledge the relativity of our moral viewpoints because they are largely formed by intuition and emotions. That is also why moral viewpoints are hard to change. Moreover, we are inclined to give morally charged viewpoints a universal meaning and to claim: That's how it should be, always and everywhere. Bridging or depolarizing opposing points of view can become especially difficult because they become part of our group identity: Us against them; our opinions and our ideology against theirs.

Developing empathy is one of the keys to this dilemma that we offer in this part of the book: Learning from each other. Empathy is the capacity to assume the position of another person, not only in their point of view (cognitive empathy), but also in their feelings (emotional empathy), or even with an active component (compassion). The most important skill you need for developing empathy is listening, in the sense of high-quality listening (or active listening). Mastering this skill—meaning really looking each other in the eye, postponing your judgment, summarizing what the other person has told you—can all lead to a development in your own thinking, not only in yourself, but also in your conversation partner. The result is that opinions and viewpoints become more flexible.

126 Part 2 Cooperation

High-quality listening is also essential for dialogue, as we have described in this part of the book. Contrary to debate, a dialogue is not meant to merely put forward contrasting views, but is essential for trying to come to an understanding with other people. Speaking and listening serve to achieve understanding and can lead to further development of different and common points of view.

Certainly, having a dialogue with another person can become very complicated. In the previous chapters we discussed how to practice dialogue with somebody else. However, dialogue within yourself is not much easier. Self-criticism and self-consultation are often needed to change your thought processes from a prior dominant position. In Part 1 we emphasized the concept of mutually opposing viewpoints. In Part 2 we wanted to show that you should also give access to the other in yourself, as another *I*-position in you, to achieve new perspectives and new points of view. Opposition is necessary, but equally important is the process of learning from one another, and from yourself.

Self-Quiz for Part 2

To strengthen your memory storage of what you have learned so far, at the end of each Part you will find a self-quiz consisting of 10 multiple-choice questions to check if you have correctly digested the background information. To pass the quiz, you need to give at least 7 correct answers to the 10 questions. If you do not pass the test, you are invited to re-examine the chapters of that Part and answer the quiz questions again. The correct answers are included in the Appendix at the end of the book. This method ensures that you get specific feedback about the level of your knowledge regarding a certain topic, and that you have mastered the content of the chapters.

Each question has four alternative answers. For each question there is only one correct or best answer. Select just one answer to each question.

1. To prevent self-criticism from undermining your feeling of self-esteem, it is necessary that self-criticism is:

   a   always task-oriented
   b   always person-oriented
   c   always motivation-oriented
   d   frequently used

2. Active (high-quality listening) has several positive consequences. Which of the occurrences below is *not* a positive consequence of active listening?

   a   subjective ambivalence
   b   objective ambivalence
   c   depolarization of opinions
   d   less defensive behavior

Epilogue to Part 2   **127**

3. Moral positions (opinions with a moral implication) more frequently lead to intolerance compared to other positions. The reason is because moral positons:

    a   are emotionally laden
    b   are based on social conventions
    c   have a universal pretension
    d   cannot be a subject of rational discussion

4. Moral opinions are often firmly anchored in the self of a person. That is why, in conversations that touch upon morally-laden issues, we can easily put up:

    a   open boundaries
    b   rigid or closed-off boundaries
    c   flexible boundaries
    d   sponge-like boundaries

5. To depolarize a moral position, two pre-conditions should be met:

    a   the person should be accountable; the topic should not be emotionally over-loaded
    b   the situation should not be emotionally loaded; there should be personal contact
    c   there should be personal contact; the topic discussed should involve a current issue
    d   the person should be accountable; there should be personal contact

6. When we reflect about contrary positions, we often encounter a master-term that is dominant and a opposite term that is not dominant. Which of the following terms are master-terms:

    a   white
    b   race
    c   homosexual
    d   emotion

7. The main advantage of debate is:

    a   participants can formulate and profile their own position
    b   participants can weaken the opinion (point of view) of their opponent
    c   participants get the opportunity to change their own viewpoint
    d   participants allow uncertainty regarding their own point of view

8. The main advantage of dialogue is:

    a   participants can formulate and profile their own point of view
    b   participants can test their point of view on its persuasiveness
    c   participants can explore a certain point of view further
    d   participants are validated regarding their point of view

128 Part 2 Cooperation

9. A "theory of mind" involves, in particular, that:

    a   someone notices the differences between their own *I*-positions

    b   someone recognizes the difference between their own perspective and that of another person

    c   someone can position themselves in the feelings of another person

    d   someone realizes that other people have their own points of view

10. Which of these examples of empathy describes this concept best:

    a   Empathy is the ability to place oneself in the position of another person

    b   Empathy is the ability to assume the perspective of people who belong to a different (social) group

    c   Empathy is the ability to experience and feel what other people feel, even though we may differ a lot from them

    d   Empathy is the ability to reduce your own insecurity

PART 3
Participation

14

FOUR LEVELS OF IDENTITY
Are You Just an Individual, or More than That?

An *I*-position is part of your self that takes shape and develops in relations you have with other people. Those other people are not only the individuals with whom you have immediate contact, such as your family members and your fellow students. We can also consider our *I*-positions or we-positions on a much wider scale—on the scale of humanity and the ecological environment. In this and the following chapters, we enlarge the scale on which we define our *I*-positions to include four levels.

From Your Own Experience

In Part 1, we examined the notion of our different *I*-positions that can be related to each other by engaging in a meta-conversation among those positions. Try to describe (again) some important *I*-positions you have.

When you introduce yourself to someone else, when you tell another person who you are, which one of those *I*-positions do you emphasize in your narrative? Or, putting it differently: Which *I*-positions do you consider as belonging to your identity, and which form the "I" of yourself? And the question that immediately arises next is: Which *I*-positions do *not* belong to your concept of your identity?

Some *I*-positions—for example, I as student, I as a Christian, I as homosexual— can indicate that you consider yourself as belonging to a certain group in society, and that you care for that group. This doesn't have to be the case with all your *I*-positions. Which are your *I*-positions or we-positions that make you a member of a particular group? Why? Of course, there can be several groups. Describe these in your own terms.

132   Part 3 Participation

Background Information

By distinguishing different "levels of inclusion," we show that the notion of "I" can be widened to "we." But we can also indicate that this "we" can be narrower or broader (Tajfel & Turner, 1979; Hermans, 2018a). On the narrowest level, I think about myself as an individual person who differs from other people and who has their own *personal identity*. On a broader level, I see myself as part of a group. On that level, the "I" becomes broadened to "we." Within that level, large differences can be observed. Some groups are smaller than others, but they can all be a part of your identity. We can manifest ourselves as a member of our family, of our class in a school setting, of a group of friends, of our sports organization, as a citizen of a city, as British, or even as European. And, as the examples indicate, these groups can be small or large. In all these cases we refer to *social identity*.

To develop a more complete identity, it is important to realize that there exists not just a personal identity (I as an individual person) plus a social identity (I as a member of a group). There is still a broader level of inclusion that has not received much attention so far in the scientific literature, but that is very important in our contemporary society, in which more and more geographical and cultural boundaries are crossed. I can perceive myself as *part of humanity* (I as a human being). In that case, I look beyond the social barriers of the specific group I belong to and I feel connected with other people, beyond social and cultural boundaries. By assuming a position on this broader level, I can feel connected with other people, not because they belong to the same group, but because they too are human beings, just like myself. In that case, we do not refer to this as group identity, but as *collective identity*. This identity, in which we refer to other persons as "human beings," makes it possible for us to cross the boundaries of group identities and to look at other people as "equals," precisely because they are human beings.

But we can still take this a step further and look at ourselves as part of the Earth. At this level, we realize that we do not just belong to groups as part of humanity, but also as part of the Earth. Viewed from this perspective, we are not "positioned" as somehow above the Earth, but we ourselves have evolved on the Earth from the organisms that have developed on our planet over the course of millions of years. On this broader level, we consider ourselves as "a part of the Earth that has become conscious of itself." This implies that we are not standing above the Earth, but are a part of it. We are "stardust." By recognizing that we are part of the planet, we also develop an *ecological identity*. The dramatic consequences of neglecting this identity are vividly described by Oreskes & Conway (2014), who look at our world from the perspective of the year 2393, when the world has become almost unrecognizable. Clear warnings of climate catastrophe went ignored for decades, resulting in rising sea levels, soaring temperatures, widespread droughts, and the "Great Collapse" in 2093.

Four Levels of Inclusion: From Smaller "I" to Broader "We"

In this chapter (and the following ones) we will pay attention to these different levels of inclusion. So far, in Parts 1 and 2 of this book, we have devoted attention to the first level (I as a music lover, I as a dreamer, I as a lover of sports) when we discussed the various *I*-positions. In the following paragraphs we will pay more attention to the other levels. All levels are coupled with *I*-positions. "I as an individual" represents the personal level, "I as member of a group" refers to the group level, "I as human being" refers to the collective level with all other human beings, and "I as part of the Earth" refers to the ecological level. We will begin with the group level.

The Minimal Group Paradigm

In social science theory, much attention is devoted to the notion of a social identity, whereby individuals come to consider themselves as part of a group. The most influential theory is "Social Identity Theory," developed by American social researchers Tajfel & Turner (1979). They discovered that it is fairly easy to make

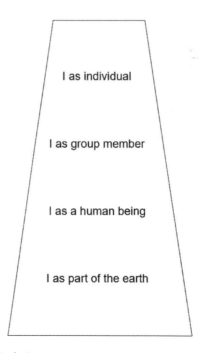

FIGURE 14.1 Levels of inclusiveness
Source: Turner et al. (1987), elaborated by Hermans (2018a)

people feel that they are members of the same group. Subjects in a research experiment were asked which paintings they liked better, those of Wassily Kandinsky or those of Paul Klee.[1] When they were divided into two groups on the basis of their preferences, a "Kandinsky group" and a "Klee group," they immediately had the *feeling* they belonged to a particular group. This occurred even in the case when, by tossing a coin, the subjects were assigned to a "heads" or "tails" group. When afterwards, the participants in the experiments were asked to allocate money, they favored the members of their own group rather than those of the other group. This phenomenon came to be known as the "paradigm of the minimal group." Even very minimal differences can cause people to think they can be distinguished from other groups and thus are willing to favor their own group above the other one.

The paradigm of the minimal group shows that individuals very quickly consider themselves as a member of a certain group, and do so on the basis of very simple difference. People who assign themselves as belonging to a certain group derive from it a certain kind of self-esteem, and the feeling that they can be distinguished in a favorable way from other people. But this paradigm only touches on superficial aspects, and the believed differences are transient. Social identities reach much deeper and are more stable when people perceive their roots as based in social and cultural differences. People differentiate themselves from other individuals in a more permanent and profound way on the basis of their cultural origin, dialect, nationality, skin color, religion, gender, or educational level. At this level, we not only see the flourishing of group identities, but we also notice that group identities can give rise to stereotyping or devaluations in judgements whereby other people are "marked off" as different, or inferior, or even as harmful to society as a whole. One's own social identity often gets rigidly barricaded, with the consequence that there is less empathy toward people who

FIGURE 14.2 Paintings by Vassily Kandinsky at the left (Source: Wikimedia Commons) and by Paul Klee (Source: Unsplash)

belong to a different ethnicity, or who hold different views about life and culture. We often characterize other individuals based on their social identity—Turkish, homosexual, over-fifty—and in doing so, we define them as people who have no other identities than those we use to characterize them.

SCHOOL SHOOTINGS AS THE ULTIMATE END OF NON-PARTICIPATION

Almost everyone wants to have a sense of belonging as part of a group: family, club, class, school, or circle of friends. Social rejection—being excluded or isolated from such groups—is one of the most painful experiences a person can undergo. The ultimate consequence of social rejection is the drama of school shootings, which shock and frighten us when we hear about them through emotional media reports. The phenomenon has attracted the interest of social scientists, who pose the question of what are the most important precursors of such shootings. A comprehensive and detailed study of the subject has been done by German investigators Sommer, Leuschner & Scheithauer (2014), who reviewed a total of 126 cases of shootings from 13 countries. They found that prior to the killings, the perpetrators of school shootings had experienced intense conflicts and problematic relations with peers and teachers, which resulted in the perpetrators' view of themselves as marginalized victims. The investigators noticed different precursors of killings: 54 percent experienced peer rejection, verbal and non-verbal; 43 percent had conflicts with teachers; 30 percent were physically bullied; and the same percentage, 30 percent, experienced romantic rejection.

From the perspective of inner democracy, one of the studies reviewed (Kimmel & Mahler, 2003) is particularly relevant. They observed that future perpetrators of school shootings failed to measure up to prevailing norms of masculinity. Almost all of 29 perpetrators analyzed in their study had been accused of being gay because they were not "tough enough." This finding suggests that most of the shootings could be understood as a violent response to what the perpetrators sensed as an attack on their masculinity.

What is the implication of these results for inner democracy? Apparently, the behavior of the shooters' peers (fellow students) was an expression of "I as tough" as a prominent or even dominating I-position in their repertoire, with the simultaneous neglect or even suppression of opposite positions such as "I as vulnerable," "I as sensitive," or "I as compassionate." This means that the rigid boundaries of their tough position prevented them from identifying with the weaker position of their schoolmates so that the experience of the victim in this situation was, at least temporarily, inaccessible. The problem is not that the peers had a tough position in their repertoire, as this position is potentially useful in other situations. It would also be a misunderstanding to think that this position should be "removed" from their repertoire. The challenge of

> inner democracy is to be able to develop the flexibility to move from a tough position to a more compassionate position that allows potential perpetrators to stand in the shoes of the other and behave accordingly.
>
> Another finding in Sommer et al.'s (2014) study is also relevant to inner democracy: They discovered the existence of *discrepancies* between their self-appraisals and the appraisals given by others. Perpetrators were described as "loners" or "social outcasts" in 47.8 percent of cases. In contrast to these external definitions, only in 23.9 percent of cases did perpetrators describe themselves as loners. Apparently, perpetrators defined themselves as loners less often than others described them as such. From this discrepancy, we may learn that when somebody looks like a "loner," they are not necessarily so in their own experience. The externally observable behavior of a person is not enough to draw conclusions about their personal experience of their personal position in the group. We don't know their personal perception. The best response to a lack of knowledge of a person's experience is not to observe and conclude—but to approach and ask!

The advantage of a group identity is that it gives us the feeling of belonging to something. Most of all, it fosters our self-esteem when we can say: I am different and better than they are. A disadvantage is that we often disqualify the members of the other group, and don't easily acknowledge them as "people like us." Here we run into the question of how to cross these barriers. In Chapters 15 and 16 we will move towards a broader level of inclusion: I as a human being.

FIGURE 14.3 Distress and helplessness after a school shooting
Source: Wikimedia Commons

Summarizing

- In a society where human beings participate as citizens, there are four levels of inclusion, each with their different identities, ranging from small to broad: as an individual, as a member of a group, as a human being, and as part of the Earth.
- We can identify those levels with four different kinds of *I*-positions or we-positions: I as an individual, I as a member of a group, I as a human being, and I as part of the Earth.
- People can characterize themselves as members of a group on the basis of minimal differences. As members of a certain group they are inclined to favor their own group and evaluate their group more positively than the other groups—the groups to which they do not belong.

Critical Questions

This is the first of three chapters exploring a more extensive notion of identity. We started with the premise that we have both an individual and a social identity. What do you think of the following statement?

> "Your identity is a compilation of individual and social *I*-positions, and the latter are formed primarily by the groups you belong to."

Maybe you think this is just a facet of your identity? What can be added to it? Or do you think nothing should be added to it? What do you think would encompass your identity?

In the text, we described the paradigm of the minimal group. Your preference for a particular artist, or even the tossing of a coin, can determine to which group you belong, a group in which members favor their own members.

Do you recognize this phenomenon? Have you ever experienced this, for example in a school situation where students are divided into groups? How does this relate to various social identities?

Exercise

Look back at what you have written under "From Your Own Experience." In that exercise you wrote which of your *I*-positions you thought would be characteristic of a certain group. Put them in order of importance. In your day-to-day life, do you ascribe different personality characteristics to the groups you think you belong to, compared with other groups? If so, why and how? (Think about the way you relate to members of those groups, how you think and feel about them.) Do you think you can track down those difference to the social identity of

138 Part 3 Participation

your own group and the other group? Or do you recognize differences between how you relate to people from your own group compared with people from other groups?

When do you think it is justified to act, think, and/or feel differently about people from another social group? And when not?

We suggest that you discuss this exercise with the other participants in your group. Look back at the instructions for how to start a dialogue in Chapter 12.

We all are members of multiple groups, and we all have multiple social *I*-positions or we-positions. You are a student, but also a family member, or a transgender person, or… How do think these social *I*-positions relate to each other? Are some more dominant, or is one more important than the others? Do they complement each other, or are they in conflict with each other? Try to arrange a conversation between two of those *I*-positions that seem to be opposed to each other (see Chapter 4). What do those *I*-positions learn from each other? Can they live peacefully with each other?

Reflecting

We want to ask you to think about the following questions in the coming weeks and months:

- What possibilities do you envision in connecting yourself with a person of another group who, according to you, has a completely different social identity from yourself? Which individual do you choose, and for what reasons?
- What are the hurdles you need to overcome when you want to establish a relationship with a person of that other group? What are the difficulties you encounter?

Note

1. Both painters were members of the abstract Cubist movement.

15

FROM GROUP IDENTITY TO HUMAN IDENTITY

What Does it Mean when You Call Yourself "Human"?

In Chapter 14 we focused on social or group identity. In this chapter we are going to approach the issue of our *I*-positions or we-positions from our identity as a human being. Do you consider yourself as a "human being"? If so, what does it mean for your relationships with other people who belong to other groups?

From Your Own Experience

All of us know that we are human beings. But do you experience "I as a human being" also as something that connects you with fellow human beings, just as a social identity connects you with other individuals? In what way, and in which situations, do you feel you are connected with other people, regardless of the group they belong to? Can you describe this in a few sentences?

At the end Chapter 14 we asked you if you could find ways to relate to other people with a different social identity. Would it be possible for you to feel connected with other people because they are all human beings, despite their gender, nationality, or skin color?

Background Information

To better understand and apply the framework of inclusion, it is important to recognize the distinction between the levels of inclusion and their differences. It is also important to realize that we can move back and forth from one level to another.

Using the model of levels of inclusion has the advantage that you can switch from one *I*-position to another without relinquishing either one of them. When you can make that transition, it turns out that one and the same event will have a different meaning for you, as you look at it from different *I*-positions.

140   Part 3 Participation

THE PIANIST

The movie *The Pianist* (2002), directed by Roman Polanski, tells the historical story of the Polish pianist Szpilman during World War II. He manages to escape deportation to a concentration camp by hiding in the ruins of the heavily destroyed city of Warsaw. At the end of the movie, we see a very moving scene in which the pianist is discovered by a German Nazi officer. When this officer asks Szpilman if he is a Jew, he answers affirmatively. Then the officer asks him what he does for a living and Szpilman answers: "I am a pianist." The officer then invites him to come with him to an adjacent space where a piano stands and asks him to play something. After some hesitation, the pianist sits down at the piano and, in that macabre environment, we hear a beautiful ballad by Chopin. The officer listens, goes away and returns later with a small food package for the pianist. The officer also gives the pianist his coat against the cold. The film is moving not only because of the surrealistic contrast between the desolate character of the ruins and the sublime quality of the music, but also because a common aesthetic experience can cause people to make a transition from sharply demarcated boundaries to a more universal human identity (Hermans, 2018, p. 135).

Difference between Group Identity and Identity as a Human Being

This difference in meaning as viewed from different viewpoints was demonstrated by the psychologists Wohl & Branscombe (2005). They were interested in situations in which people showed a more or less forgiving attitude after they, or members of their group, had suffered serious maltreatment or injustice. The researchers wondered if it would make a difference if you let people look at something from the perspective of group identity or from the perspective of their identity as a human being ("I as a human being"). They invited a group of Jewish American people to look back at their collective past and to express their thoughts about the Holocaust. A first group of Jewish subjects in this experiment were given a text which described how inhumanely the Germans behaved toward Jewish people. In this part of the research, the subjects were approached in terms of their *social identity as Jews*. A second group of Jewish subjects were given a text in which the Holocaust was described in more general terms, as an event where one group of people had behaved in an aggressive way toward another group of people. In the second version, both the perpetrators as well as the victims were described in relation to their *identity as human beings*. Afterward, both groups were asked to indicate to what degree Germans should feel guilty about the atrocities of their ancestors. It turned out that the subjects in the second group, who had looked at the Holocaust from their identity as human beings, were less accusing than the subjects in the first group, who described this event in terms of group identity. These results were not specific to the experiences of Jews. When the researchers repeated the same procedure for a group of Native Canadian people who had experienced a history of aggression and cultural genocide, the same results were found. Both research results showed that people are more forgiving when they take the position of *I*-as-a-human-being than when they identify themselves in terms of their group identity. This research shows that the same event can be seen from different *I*-positions, and this has consequences for the way we evaluate that event.

Leadership in a Globalizing World

To understand the position of "I as a human being," we can use an example of some leaders who have played a historically prominent role in situations of group conflict. An article written by journalist Bas Heijne (2018), entitled "The radical answer to hate is dignity," is worth reading in this context. He carried out research about the similarities between three world leaders: Gandhi, King, and Mandela.

Mahatma Gandhi viewed identity as a solid building, a safe space where one can feel at home, but a home with wide-open shutters. According to Gandhi, there is not just a religious, cultural, and social identity, but also something like a human identity that connects individuals and groups with each other, despite their differences. Although he was Hindu, he was very much intrigued by Christianity and Islam, and he wanted to cross the borders between these different religions.

According to Heijne, a similar attitude can be seen in Nelson Mandela. Despite everything that was done to him, he showed a huge interest in the culture and history of the Afrikaners, and he encouraged his fellow Anti-apartheid comrades to do the same. As a leader he was able, after centuries of conflict and war between population groups, to build bridges between black and white people.

Another icon, Martin Luther King Jr, pointed out that whoever answers hate with hate runs the risk of behaving as the mirror image of the person who suppresses them. There comes a moment when reason and moral acknowledgement are required for breaking through the chain of hatred.

At the end of the article, Heijne concludes that there is a connection between societal and individual development: All three—Gandhi, King, and Mandela—were convinced that prejudices are the source of discrimination and inequality. And from their own upbringing, they knew too that not only were prejudices aimed *at* them, but prejudices also existed *in* them. It is this wall that needs to be broken down, Martin Luther King said. And he added that changing society is not the most difficult thing to do; the most difficult thing is changing yourself. In a world in which several forces are in conflict with each other, this is a quest that is as difficult as it is real.

142 Part 3 Participation

From the lessons that Gandhi, King, and Mandela left us, we learn that there are moments in life when we need to transcend the attachment we feel to our group identities. The flexibility to change from individual and group positions to the position "I as a human being" offers a basis for the position "I as a citizen of the world," which is necessary to participate as a democratic citizen in a globalizing society.

Locking a Minority Group into One Exclusive Identity

It can happen that we look at members of a certain group solely as members of that group, and that we have no eye for the fact that they too are individuals, with their own characteristics and peculiarities. This might occur when we look at immigrants, or people with a different skin color or cultural heritage, as representing only *one* distinct group. Suppose you read in the news about a crime committed by an immigrant. We might spontaneously ascribe a certain crime not just to this particular individual, but consider it as a characteristic of *all* members of the group (again those F*** Mexicans!). When the same crime is committed by a white American, then we proclaim that this is just an act of an *individual* culprit. Here we become aware of a biased identity determination that in fact says more about the person who utters it than about the person toward whom it is directed. As a consequence of this biased moral judgment, someone who has not committed a crime is forced into the position of having to defend themselves against those accusations. In this way, people from the group that is discriminated

FIGURE 15.1 One group, yet very different individuals
Wikimedia Commons

against become locked into an exclusive (not inclusive) position on the group identity level.

Cultural anthropologist Toon van Meijl (2020) has observed that people from non-western origins often complain that they are considered as solely members of the social group to which they belong, but not as individuals. They feel frustrated because they are addressed only in relation to their ethnicity or religion, and are therefore characterized as "as different from us." At the same time, they long to be considered not only as representatives of their own group, but also as cosmopolitan citizens. And so van Meijl advocates that we change the way we position "foreigners": Away from an emphasis on exclusive group identities and toward communal citizenship in a border-crossing society.

van Meijl emphasizes that, in the case of the identity of immigrants, we should see them not just as representatives of their group, but also as individuals with their own characteristics, desires, and wishes, just as we all have. Because the self of a person can be viewed as a "mini-society of *I*-positions," he proposes that we should take into consideration the diversities of those positions. There are more positions in each individual than just the position of an immigrant. They also have other positions in which they are similar to us, such as "I as a parent," "I as a neighbor," "I as a colleague," "I as a fan of a football club," etc. In these positions both they *and* we can experience significant similarities and meet each other without getting stuck in the "we versus they" identities of exclusive distinctions. And instead of our inclination to lock immigrants into their exclusive ethnic or religious identities, we need to think more broadly about them as representatives of different groups (as a parent in a family, as a person who lives in our neighborhood). We can also find commonality by considering them as individuals (as a lover of music), and as human beings (as citizens who participate in global society). Acknowledging multiple identities in other individuals, linked to different levels of inclusion, is necessary to correct stereotyping and prejudices in relation to minority groups in our society.

The Coronavirus Pandemic and the Confusion of Levels of Inclusion

The recent coronavirus pandemic demonstrates that the different levels of inclusion should be carefully distinguished. Confusion occurs when a particular problem is identified at one level, when it should be placed at another level. *New York Times* opinion columnist Bouie (2020) presents statistics showing that Covid-19 is killing African Americans at faster rates than any other group. As a response to this problem, Federal officials have tied these disparities to *individual* behavior, and urged blacks and other individuals of color to avoid alcohol, tobacco, and drugs as particular problems in those groups. In this way, it is suggested that the greater rates of deaths among African Americans is a problem that has to be resolved at the individual level only, without taking into account the historical precedents that are found at the group level. In truth, Bouie argues, black susceptibility to infection and death in the pandemic has everything to do with the racial character of inequality in the United States. For example, black Americans are more likely to work in service sector jobs, they are least likely to own their home, and least likely to own a car. Therefore they are more likely to be in close contact with other people, given the way they travel, the kinds of work they do, and the conditions in which they live. Bouie argues that the differences of health have their roots in yesterday's disparities of wealth and opportunity. The over-representation of African Americans in service sector jobs is the result of a long history of racially segmented labor markets that placed them at the bottom of the economic ladder. Their lack of home ownership has its roots in a history of stark housing discrimination. Therefore Bouie concludes that, if black Americans are more likely to suffer from conditions that make coronavirus more deadly, it's because those conditions are connected to the segregation and concentrated poverty that still mark their communities today.

As this example demonstrates, the greater likelihood of coronavirus death in the black community is a problem that has a long history at the group level. If governments want to improve people's life conditions, they should take into account the systematic discrimination that has plagued the history of the United States over the past centuries. This requires a distinction between the different levels of inclusion. Reducing the problem to the individual level would be confusing, because any behavior at the individual level has its historical precedents at the group level. At the same time, this example demonstrates that in order to correct racial discrimination, it is essential to move from the group level to the human level of inclusion, as discrimination can be effectively corrected only if different racial, ethnic, religious, and gender groups are all acknowledged as human beings and morally treated as equals. Therefore, any societal problem with identity implications requires an analysis of the different levels of inclusion and their careful distinction as a basis of political decision making.

Summarizing

- It is possible to switch from "I as a member of a group" to "I as a human being."
- This switch makes it possible to evaluate a certain event in different ways.
- Great leaders have taught us that participating in global society requires that one should not describe a person only as belonging to a certain group, but also as a human being or a citizen of the world.
- Commonality with people from other cultures can flourish by regarding them not just as representatives of their specific group, but also as individuals and world citizens, just as we are.

Critical Questions

In the text we argue that a part of our humanity also forms our identity, a collective identity. What are your thoughts about this? Is this a matter of identity? If this applies to all human beings, then are we not really different from each other? Or are we?

In the text, three people are described who have played a significant role in history: Gandhi, King, and Mandela. In your opinion, what are the extraordinary qualities of these three men? And do these qualities make them "superhuman," or could anybody develop such qualities? Would you consider these three men as examples of people who have developed an inner democracy? Or do you think they are not so special?

Exercise

We are inclined to ascribe an individual act, committed by a person from a group we do not like, to the entire group, and to proclaim this as a defining characteristic of that group. We tend to view other people who belong to such a group as rather one-dimensional: He is homosexual, she is a Moroccan. Prejudices toward such groups are associated with negative characteristics that we ascribe to all members of the group. These are stubborn mechanisms that most of us can overcome only by regular practicing and reflection. To view human beings who belong to another group as, indeed, human beings and not just as members of a group, we propose the following exercise. It is a variation on the exercise we described in Chapter 13.

- Think of someone you only, or especially, know as homosexual, as Muslim, as Mexican, as … What is their name? Write their name on a piece of paper and draw a line from the name to the first position: e.g., he or she as transgender.
- Now think about the other *I*-positions that person has, or—in case you are not so familiar with this person—that they might have. Which *I*-positions can you identify and ascribe to this person on an individual level, and which *I*-positions on a group identity level?
- Can you also see this person as a human being? If so, what is the difference between seeing this person as a representative of a group, or as an individual?

Reflecting

- You can do Exercise 2 in your thoughts, or when walking in the streets, or riding the subway. Look around, select somebody. What other I-positions

146 Part 3 Participation

does this person have? Can you break through your dominant stereotypes with this practice?

- Under "From Your Own Experience" you looked for ways to reach out to others beyond their group identity. Read again the story about the pianist and the Nazi officer. Better yet, see the movie and hear the music. This is an extreme example in every aspect. But can we learn something from it: Why does the Nazi officer reach beyond his group identity to a communal human identity?

- We have described how an aesthetic experience (such as listening to beautifully played music) can cause a transformation in certain attitudes. This is the catalyst that prompts the officer in his specific behavior towards the pianist. Are there catalysts in your life that make it possible to reach beyond conflicting identities and connect as a human being with other human beings?

16

ARE WE MASTERS OF THE EARTH OR PART OF IT?

In this chapter we move to the fourth level of identity: Being part of the Earth. How do we consider our ecological environment? Is it something that is simply there to serve us? Do we stand above the physical Earth as something that belongs to an external realm, or is it part of our own identity? If so, what kind of responsibility do we have?

From Your Own Experience

Ecological problems are continually imposed on us, and concerns about climate change are the most pressing. What are your thoughts about this issue? Is it something you feel involved with or maybe feel responsible for? Or do you think it is a serious problem, but something you cannot solve? Or do you think this climate change problem is made much bigger than it is, and we should not worry so much about it? Can you describe this in a few sentences?

Background Information

To differentiate between the levels of inclusion, see Figure 14.1. As we described there, in contact with other people we should not get stuck solely in a form of *individualism*, or in a form of *group thinking* in which one group is glorified at the expense of another group. We saw that observing people and reaching out to them as *human beings* makes it possible to look beyond the borders of both the individual and group levels to which we belong. In this chapter, we take an additional step in our thought process. We are not only human among other human beings, but we are also *part of the Earth*. This level of inclusion is necessary at a time when our relation to the Earth is more than ever under discussion.

148   Part 3 Participation

The Actuality of Ecological Awareness

In connection with participation, people in our society are becoming more and more aware of the importance of our environment and the habitability of our planet. Since the alarming report *The limits to growth* (Meadows et al., 1972), people have realized that we human beings are partly responsible for many ecological problems, as is also clear from the recent discussions about climate change.

MUSIC AS SPREADING A NEW MORALITY

As you may know, the English DJ Fatboy Slim mixed his song "Right Here, Right Now" with the speech Greta Thunberg gave at the 2019 UN Climate Action Summit in New York. Inspired by this mixture, St. Paul, the artist name of the Dutch DJ Paul Nederveen, made his own version of the song and commented:

> "In a very clear way, he [Fatboy Slim] has made a statement and pop music has always been a place for catchy stories" and he continues: "I consider it as healthy when people are forced to look at things in a different way. In this manner I look at everything, from Black Peter [the controversial helper of St. Nicholas in the Netherlands' tradition] to climate. When you look at it, do you think 'what can I contribute?' Or do you say: 'They take something away from me?' In my view, this is a simple choice. The nice thing is that this all is happening in the public space. Together you are inventing a new morality, also in your club"
>
> *(Nederveen, 2019)*

In their study of climate change and pop culture, Boykoff, Goodman, and Littler (2010), researchers in the area of environmental governance, observe that celebrities have become the new "charismatic megafauna" for climate awareness. In so doing, these "actors" have taken climate change from distant places and brought it into our living environments and even into our private living rooms. In this context, they praise the UK organization "Global Cool," a climate change charity that aims not only to raise awareness of climate change but also to provide practical solutions for its mitigation. One of the more unique initiatives by Global Cool was to get the DJ Erik Prydz to support them with a music video entitled "Proper Education" featuring a remix of Pink Floyd's "Another Brick in the Wall." This music was paired with school kids who were, in a public-housing estate, secretly installing compact florescent bulbs into the flats of residents. At the end of the video, a tag-line appears: "You don't need a proper education to save the planet."

In recent public discussions on to what degree human behavior is responsible, more or less, for the causes of climate change, an increasing number of people (scientists and governments) are aware that the warming of the Earth will have enormous consequences for the future of the planet and thus for humanity. It has become more and more a question of how we can deal with issues such as driving cars with high CO_2 emissions, frequent air travel causing air pollution, living in badly insulated houses, and eating unlimited amounts of meat. We can no longer take this kind of behavior for granted and ignore this complex problem—we need to permanently change our behavior.

As an individual consumer, you could do whatever you wanted (under the proviso you had enough money), but now a situation has been created in which we find ourselves in a tension field between two *I*-positions: I as a consumer, and I as a citizen in a boundary-crossing environment. Both *I*-positions are accompanied by a responsibility. As a consumer, I need to take care materially of myself and other people. As a citizen, I need to take care of the environment, my fellow human beings in other parts of the world, and the future of our children and ourselves. Here we are placed in a tension field that causes uncertainty and invites us to an inner dialogue between our position as a consumer and our position as a citizen. This dialogue leads to a decision that determines which *I*-position prevails at that moment and in that situation.

This example illustrates what it means to find yourself in a tension field between multiple *I*-positions that invites us to have dialogues with ourselves and with other people. When we look at this situation from different perspectives of inclusion, then we notice that we are placed at multiple levels at the same time. As consumers, we are primarily at the individual level. We are consumers because we want to take care of ourselves and people in our immediate environment. As citizens, we are placed at a group level, for example, I as a citizen of my own country, but also as a world citizen whereby we are part of humanity. As a world citizen, we are also members of the ecological stratum when we feel alarmed by pollution that takes place across country boundaries. And thus we are invited to move from one level to another, and our behavior is influenced by the various relations between those levels. At this point, the level of I as a human being is especially important. As a citizen of the world, concerned with the fate of other human beings, it is necessary that I assume not just a group position that favors my own group at the expense of the well-being of other people, but also a position as a human being that includes the welfare of other people. The current situation of environmental issues requires that we take care of our natural environment.

Our position as part of the ecological system has been discussed profoundly by science journalist Sonia Shah (2016) in her book *Pandemic: Tracking contagions from cholera to Ebola and beyond*. In a recent interview, in which she reflected on the

150 Part 3 Participation

coronavirus outbreak, she comments that we are insufficiently aware of the fact that all life on Earth, including that of the human being, is part of the same ecosystem (Somers, 2020). Shah reminds us that we have not realized, or do not want to realize, that most pandemics are related to the destruction of ecosystems that exist as the natural environments in which we participate. We have neglected to reserve sufficient place for wild animals:

> "Not only do we stand at the beginning of a possibly catastrophic biodiversity crisis, also we facilitate the transmission of viruses among animals and from animals to humans, because we crowd animals too much together. Other animals, like birds and amphibians, were already the target of plagues. Now it also hits humans worldwide."
>
> *(Somers, 2020; author's translation)*

Statements like this make us aware of the reality that we are *part of a network of natural systems* from which we cannot separate ourselves.

More than ever, the current world situation asks us to differentiate between the various levels of inclusion and to show our willingness to take all those levels of inclusion into consideration when we decide what behavior pattern we should assume. This requires a certain amount of *flexibility* in moving from the smaller position of an individual and group member, to we as human beings and we as part of the Earth, and then to return to the more restricted level of individual *I*-positions with the question: How do I react in a situation that involves new and bigger ecological challenges? Being aware of those various different positions leads us to the core of our inner democracy: We need to acknowledge all the various and different positions that play a role in situations that are relevant for the protection of our ecological environment.

Our Responsibilities

In his influential book *Adaptation to climate change*, English climate researcher Mark Pelling (2011) argues that in the current climate discussion, one important democratic value stands above all: Fairness as a form of justice. He demonstrates that justice in a situation of climate change requires a link between the ecological level (I as part of the Earth) and the collective level (I as a human being).

Pelling develops his theory about fairness along three lines of reasoning:

- Acceptance of the points of view of minority groups when making decisions and planning in a situation of climate problems. This means that we need to take into account the most marginalized and vulnerable groups in society. These are people who live in regions of the world that in the future will be confronted with everlasting drought, or the risks of devastating flooding.

Are We Masters of the Earth or Part of It? 151

TABLE 16.1 Different levels of inclusiveness

I-position	Description	Responsibility
I as an individual	I present myself as an individual and as different from other people	Individual
I as a group member	I present myself as a group member and as different from other groups	Social
I as a human being	I present myself as a human being and include other groups	Collective
I as part of the Earth	I present myself as part of the Earth that becomes aware of itself	Ecological

- Access to information and knowledge about all relevant aspects of climate change, so that all groups that may be affected by it can be included in future decision making.
- Dissemination of information about who has the power in the decision-making process, so that the weakest and most vulnerable individuals in our society can participate in this process.

We can also see these indications about fairness in the tension field between the three levels. They can be found on the ecological level; they involve vulnerable groups in the decision-making process (group level); and they appeal to our position as a human being and world citizen (collective level). A fair society requires that these different perspectives, specific to the different levels of inclusion, are interwoven with each other.

Taken together, we can distinguish four responsibilities that are correlated with different levels of inclusion. *Individual responsibility* concerns our own well-being and care for our self. When the individual position receives too much emphasis at the expense of other individuals, then phenomena such as egocentrism and narcissism can arise, which are sometimes considered as "epidemics" of our time. Then there is *social responsibility* that requires taking care of the groups we feel affiliated with. This level is important for groups that are in a process of emancipation (e.g., gay and transgender individuals). However, in some situations group thinking can lead to extreme behavior. We see this in certain forms of nationalism and populism in which people react in an offensive way against issues such as immigration and climate change. And then there is the level of *collective responsibility*, that asks us to take care of the most vulnerable individuals and groups in the world as a whole. After all, we have an *ecological responsibility* for the wellbeing of the Earth on which we evolved, and that more than ever is suffering the consequences of our own behavior.

Summarizing

- In a society in which people participate as citizens, there are four levels of inclusion with different identities, varying from narrow to wide: I as an individual, I as a member of a group, I as a human being, and I as a part of the Earth.
- Those levels correspond to four levels of responsibility: Individual, social, collective, and ecological responsibility.
- To develop a democratic self that can participate in wider society, we need to be able to move in a flexible way from one level to another, dependent on the situation in which we find ourselves.

Critical Questions

We have made a huge step forward in this chapter. What do you think of presenting yourself as part of the Earth? Do you think this is part of your identity? How does this relate to your various *I*-positions?

FIGURE 16.1 Caring for the Earth
Source: Wikimedia Commons

Dutch philosopher Chris Bremmers (2019) argues that the issue of the durability of the Earth is too abstract and too "far away" for many people to become seriously involved with. According to him, a human being needs as close a connection with the Earth as they have with other fellow human beings. The question he asks is: How can we become more concerned about such world problems? He thinks that symbolism can be useful in this respect, such as the use of photos, paintings, sculptures, film, or other art forms. How do you think we can achieve a close relationship with world problems, especially when the implications seem so far away from us? Think of important problems, such as climate, robotics, migration.

Exercise

In this book we assume that other people can be part of ourselves. This manifests itself in our different *I*-positions. When we discuss our relationships with family and friends, this is easily recognizable. But what about the ecology of the Earth: How does this function in your *I*-positions? You will probably have a harder time recognizing this aspect—or maybe not?

Think about people or objects that have a strong presence in you: A tree, a landscape, a favorite aspect of nature, an animal. Describe (via brainstorming) the different ways in which this aspect of the environment is present in you and is a part of you. Make a list of the different characteristics that appeal to you. In case it is difficult for you to do this, the following examples might help you:

- think about a moment of beauty when you were in a natural environment
- think about a family member or friend who made you aware of the beauty of nature
- think about behavioral acts of other people who were inspired to take care of our natural environment and inspired you to do something similar.

Do you now think in the same way about how the natural environment is situated in yourself: How your thought processes, your emotions, and your behavior are also determined by concern about nature? Which of your *I*-positions are particularly related to the environment and the Earth? How do they relate to the social identities that you have described in Chapter 14 (similarities, differences, dilemmas)?

In "From Your Own Experience" you formulated your view on climate problems. How do you look at this now, at the end of the chapter? Would you change or expand your original statement? If not, could you explain why the text and exercises did not make any difference for you?

FIGURE 16.2 How precious is biodiversity?
Source: Wikimedia Commons

Reflecting

In the exercises above we focused on two questions that are hard to answer. We invite you to think about these questions from time to time in the coming weeks and months.

- Which of your *I*-positions are especially related to the Earth?
- What, in your view, are possible ways to connect to areas in the world that are not part of your immediate environment?
- Do you see a connection with the problem of threatened biodiversity?

17

HOW CAN WE PROMOTE INNER DEMOCRACY?

In Chapters 17 and 18, we will address what factors can promote or obstruct inner democracy. The point is that the development of inner democracy requires that a person should be able to let a diversity of *I*-positions *participate* in contact with other people and with the other *I*-positions in themselves. In this chapter we describe some factors that promote this participation: Developing a "dialogical capacity," being able to set boundaries, and the acknowledgement of multi-voicedness, not just in ourselves but also in the other person. Then in Chapter 18 we will discuss some obstructing factors.

From Your Own Experience

When you have a conversation with other people, you can assume various positions. You can open your boundaries, or you can close off the boundaries of your position. Preferably your boundaries are not too open (they become soft) or too closed (they become rigid). It is best to assume a *flexible* position-repertoire, in which you know what your position is while being open to embracing alternative viewpoints (Chapter 4). What do you think—can you succeed in taking this attitude in your conversations with other people?

Try to remember a conversation, preferably a somewhat difficult conversation, from not so long ago. Try to reconstruct this conversation: When did you open yourself up and why, and at what point did you perhaps go too far with this attitude? When did you form a barricade around your position and why, and when did you take this "closed-off" position too far? Write this down in a few sentences.

Do you ever have a dialogue with yourself, between two or more *I*-positions? What was your experience regarding open, closed, or flexible positions? It is

156 Part 3 Participation

probably not as easy to answer this question as the previous question. When you put your *I*-positions somewhat at a distance, it becomes easier to contemplate them: I the student, in a conversation with I the friend, or I the angry person, or I who wants to have contact with somebody. Who is open here? Who shuts themself off? Or can you take a flexible position in moving yourself from a closing position to opening up yourself or, the other way around, from opening up to closing off yourself? Do you notice when and why this is not an easy thing to do, and when and why it is easy to do so? Write this down in a few sentences.

Background Information

Inner democracy is not a "given." Just like democracy at large, it needs to be protected and activated, and requires insight into both the factors that promote it and the factors that obstruct it. In this chapter we concentrate on some factors that can promote inner democracy.

In its broadest sense, we are continuously involved with dialogical relations. This happens when we participate in a question-and-answer conversation. We then make use of verbal and non-verbal signs to make ourselves understood by others when conveying a message. This is more or less obvious. It becomes somewhat more difficult to understand this process when we realize that dialogue doesn't just relate to situations in which we are in agreement with someone else, but also to situations in which we disagree with one another. Only then does dialogue become an intriguing process. In Chapter 12 we indicated that being in disagreement with one another in a productive way is much harder than being in agreement. It can be painful if our opinions do not receive the confirmation we would like. A fruitful dialogue requires that we tolerate this painful moment and continue with the conversation, even if our opinion does not get the agreement we would like. And we strive for that agreement because it enhances our self-esteem. We also observed that it is sometimes necessary to offer a small "sacrifice" in the form of a temporary reduction of our feeling of self-esteem. This occurs when, as a result of the disagreement, we have to correct ourselves and learn something that was not there before. The temporary reduction of our self-esteem is then rewarding because it results in a new insight.

The question is, what do we expect from a good dialogue? If we aim solely for self-confirmation, then it is obvious that we look for situations in which our opinions get strengthened, and look for people who confirm our currently held opinions. But if we want to learn something new, or even something that is contrary to our own point of view, then it is necessary that we put aside our own viewpoint for a little while and open up to something that goes against our own initial opinion. That is why we emphasized the importance of *postponement of judgment* (Chapter 3) for a constructive dialogue with another person. When we hear something we disagree with, our first impulse is to defend our original point of view. If we take the position of a hedgehog, then the (new) information from somebody else does not reach us, because we are, at that moment, rather busy seeing things from our own perspective and not from someone else's. We can no longer position ourselves in the experiential world of the other person. And because that positioning is so important for entering into a dialogue, we paid special attention to the capacity to feel *empathy* as a precondition of dialogue (Chapter 13). We elaborated this concept by making a distinction between different forms of empathy—cognitive, emotional, and compassion—that make it possible to enter the world of the other person, to pay attention to it, and use it in a constructive way. In short, suspending our own judgment, overcoming our impulsive defensive responses in a situation of disagreement, and developing our empathetic capability are necessary components of our dialogical capacity. When these factors are absent, this capacity is not present or is underdeveloped. But when these factors are present, we are capable of gaining access to the inner world of another person. Moreover, we enter a world that is different from our own but might offer the possibility of broadening our overall view. To make this happen, more factors need to be included, and this involves the process of opening and closing off the boundaries of our inner self.

Opening Up and Closing Off Our Mental Boundaries

Our dialogical capacity depends for a large part on our own psychological boundaries. We have already discussed the theme of drawing boundaries between yourself and the other person in Part 1, but here we delve more deeply into this issue because of its relevant implications for inner democracy.

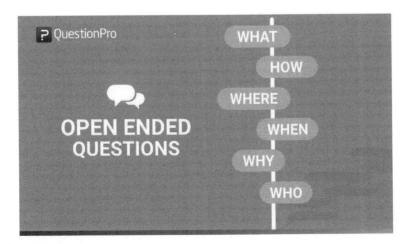

FIGURE 17.1 Open questions are indispensable for a constructive dialogue
Source: Wikimedia Commons

158 Part 3 Participation

Putting up boundaries for self-protection is already noticeable in children's early development. As early as their first year, children learn to develop a "personal space" in which they feel safe. Just after birth that space is not yet present, but after a few of months we start to notice that children feel comfortable when their mother comes close and touches them, but they become afraid when a stranger does so. If the stranger comes too close, the child turns away, and they start to frown and scream if the other enters their safety zone. We also see this phenomenon of personal space and its boundaries in adolescence and later. Developmental researchers Burgoon & Jones (1976), who studied this phenomenon, describe personal space as "an invisible, dynamic, and transportable space" with which people surround themselves and that they constantly carry around with them. That space is dynamic because in some situations it becomes smaller (e.g., in an elevator) and in other environments larger (e.g., in a forest). To better understand the concept of drawing boundaries in the relations between myself and the other, clinical psychologist Nina Brown (2006) differentiated between four boundaries: soft, rigid, sponge-like, and flexible. The latter form is best for developing a dialogical capability, as we will show here (see also Hermans, 2018).

Soft Boundaries

The boundaries of the self are soft when the person is not capable of closing them at a moment when it is necessary. This happens when people are not able to rely on themselves in situations in which they have to be assertive, or have to defend themselves against other individuals. Let's look at the example of people who can be characterized as overdependent. They find it difficult to make decisions on their own, and come to rely upon someone else who tells them what to do or not to do. They look for protection from somebody else, who is taking the initiative. The result is that they become gradually more and more dependent and can no longer stand on their own feet. Soft boundaries between oneself and another individual can also be found in people who react in an "over-emphatic" way to other people. They position themselves so strongly in the psychological sphere of another person that they get "sucked into" the feelings and emotions of the other person. They can no longer create a distance between themselves and other people, and so it becomes difficult to advise or help them. Think about two people having a conversation in which they share only pessimistic thoughts or beliefs about the terrible situation they are in. You might notice something similar in charismatic schoolteachers who give students advice and support to such an extent that the student becomes overly dependent on their teacher. In such a teacher–student relation, the boundaries are absent or too soft.

Rigid Boundaries

The boundaries of the self become rigid when they remain closed, even in situations where there is no convincing reason to do so. Imagine a couple who end up in a divorce situation because they each think their partner has treated them unjustly. After the divorce there may be every reason to make the relationship better, especially in the interests of the children. However, sometimes couples continue to blame one another and are not prepared to discuss their own role in this situation. They believe that the blame lies completely with the other person. They refuse to improve contact or to create a situation of even minimal understanding. We also see this sometimes in the teacher–student relationship, when a student feels so upset by a bad rating that they build up rigid boundaries towards the teacher. The student feels victimized because of the teacher's rating, and can no longer maintain an open attitude towards the teacher.

Sponge-like Boundaries

These boundaries are somewhat harder to understand, even though we frequently observe them. We find them in relationships where someone both feels dependent on someone else and at the same time struggles to keep their own autonomy. Sons or daughters may feel as if they behave just like their parents, but at the same do not want to be like them. In such a case, the son or daughter identifies themself with one of their parents, but at the same time wants to disengage from them. It can also happen in relations with a family member or with a boy- or girlfriend. Confusion arises when it is no longer clear where one's own position is: Are you independent or not? When you make a decision, is that something coming from you yourself, or more from "the other in yourself"? Self and other are mixed here. We also observe sponge-like responses in our day-to-day interactions with other people. They occur when someone gives a vague response to a question, with no clear distinction between yes or no. Are you coming to my party? The invitee says "yes," but at the same time feels "no." The person who asks the question notices the difference between the verbal "yes" and the non-verbal "no," resulting in a situation of confusion. Neither party then knows how to make sense of it.

Flexible Boundaries

We speak of a flexible boundary between our self and the other if the self can be open or closed depending on the situation. While people with soft boundaries cannot close themselves off when it is necessary, and people who build rigid boundaries cannot open up when the situation calls for it, a flexible person can move back and forth between opening and closing of boundaries. When they say "yes," it is yes, and when they say "no," it is no. They can do this because their decisions are formed by their own thoughts and feelings. And when they ask advice from other people, although they take other people's advice into consideration, eventually they make their own decisions. They open their boundaries in seeking contact with other people, and share things with other people. But they are capable of temporarily closing their boundaries in situations where they want to realize their own goals. We see this when a teacher is approached by a student for advice. The teacher is open and is willing to help the student. However, after a little while the teacher notices that the student is exhibiting claiming behavior and appealing to the teacher in an excessive way. From that moment on, the teacher will make it clear to the student that they cannot be available all the time and in every situation. The teacher is obliged to set up boundaries in response to the student's behavior, and to make this clear. In this case we see that the teacher is capable of opening themselves up but they respond to the claiming behavior of the student by closing their boundaries, albeit temporarily.

Boundaries in Relation to Ourselves

These different kinds of boundaries can also occur in the relations we have with ourselves. Let's consider the example of people who have trouble dealing with their own insecurity. Some situations provoke feelings of insecurity in people, and this can lead to feelings of anxiety. Some people will not admit these feelings of insecurity to themselves. As a response, they start to protest very loudly to silence this kind of insecurity. Instead of permitting these feelings and responding to them, they put up a shield and assume a pose that is more self-confident than what they actually feel. Feelings of insecurity will then not be allowed and do not get a chance to become part of one's self-reflection and inner dialogue. When an individual notices a kind of insecurity in themselves that they don't want to face, then *rigid* boundaries will be built in order to prevent these experiences.

It can also happen that the boundaries of the self are *soft*. This occurs when an individual can't control their own behavior even though they are suffering from certain aspects of their behavior. In this context, we can think of all kinds of addictions whereby a person can't keep certain aspects of their behavior under control: smoking, gambling, unhealthy eating, uncontrolled consumption, addiction to computer games, etc. These individuals have a hard time in saying: This is as far as I want to go, and no further. At that point, they find difficult or impossible to stand up against themselves.

The boundaries inside your self can also have *sponge-like* qualities. The person acknowledges that a change in behavior is required, but avoids making a decision to actually change their behavior. They prefer to leave it as it is in certain situations. When they do have to make a decision, they tell themselves: "I'll see how this works out." Their conscience is soothed with open-ended plans for the future that are never realized because decisions are constantly postponed. In such situations, we say yes and no to ourselves simultaneously, and as long as such a vague construction exists, the boundaries we deal with in ourselves will stay sponge-like, unclear, and vague.

For a more effective and also more satisfying way to deal with certain conflicts, we need to resort to flexible boundaries. At certain moments and in certain situations we open up to ourselves, and at other moments we put limits on our impulses. For example, today I'm really not feeling in the mood to study. The question is: Do I let myself be led by this impulse? No, not completely. I decide to study for two hours and then do something else. At the same time, I am making a firm plan to do what I should have done today or tomorrow. Or, I have worked really very hard for days on end and I have committed myself to a pretty heavy regime, with hardly any relaxation time. I'm now going to reward myself by doing something I really like. In this example, I put up boundaries at a certain moment, but at another moment I'm also open to things that I like. I follow my impulses at one moment, but I construct boundaries at another moment. We can look at some other examples to clarify this: I eat no more than I should and then I will stop. Or, I will be online for just this amount of time and then I'm going to do something else. At these moments, I put up boundaries that are flexible in nature.

Dialogical Capability and Forming Boundaries

We arrive now at a point where we can synchronize dialogical capability and putting up boundaries. The core of the argument is this: Dialogical relations with other people and with ourselves benefit from flexible boundaries. Why? To have an enriching dialogue with another person, two conditions need to be met. First, it is necessary to open yourself up to the opinions and arguments of the other

FIGURE 17.2 In the course of evolution, we *Homo sapiens* have become a question to ourselves—we need a flexible mind to deal with our impulses

Source: Wikimedia Commons

162 Part 3 Participation

person, and also to the emotions that are invoked within yourself. This is not easy, certainly when the opinions of the other person vary radically from your own, or are even completely contradictory to yours. Second, at the moment when you express your own point of view and the experiences that have led you to it, you need to concentrate on this endeavor, making your point clear, and not going along with other viewpoints without voicing your own opinion. You have to be very strong to utter something that the other person might not want to hear, but you still want to say it because it reflects your personal point of view and experience. When, on the contrary, you position yourself in a *soft* spot, you might be overruled by the other person's viewpoints and you will not be able to express yourself. However, every time you oppose yourself against another person, despite their efforts to gain access to your experiential world, the risk is that your own boundaries become *rigid*. The art of dialogue is that you react in a *flexible way* towards other individuals and at the same time towards yourself. In this process, your own experiences and verbal expressions and those of the other person come to the forefront alternately, and this is how you can learn from each other. That is the core of inner democracy and having a democratic relationship with other people.

The Other as Multi-voiced

In our daily life, we often make use of certain personality traits to characterize other people. In doing so, we are inclined to give a prominent place to certain characteristics while neglecting others. Someone can be seen as a "funny guy" or "leader of the gang," another person can be seen as a "really gloomy thinker," and another as "naïve." When we think that another person is "loyal" we expect that this person is "always loyal," and when we typify somebody as "untrust-worthy" we are inclined to see them as "untrustworthy in every circumstance." When we characterize somebody in a certain way, we are inclined to place a certain characteristic to the forefront and generalize this characteristic to other situations in which this person acts or might act.

Entire populations or groups are characterized according to features that the scientific literature labels as "social stereotypes." In general, these are over-simplified, highly generalized, and widely accepted ways to typify members of a particular social or cultural group. We surely know that not all Germans are hard-working people, not all Greek people are lazy hedonists, and not all Italians are charming womanizers. But still, we notice in our daily lives that such stereotypes are frequently used, and easily and almost naturally shared among people. After having characterized an individual or a group by using stereotypes, we assume that they are "really like this." We pretend to be observers of other individuals and come to see them as people "who really possesses those characteristics." This is how we often deal with "objective reality."

How Can We Promote Inner Democracy? **163**

We need to realize that our expectations resulting from our own social stereotyping also influence the people we aim to categorize: It is a reciprocal chain of events. This is certainly the case with groups of people who have a different skin color, or who dress or speak differently. When we perceive these groups as inferior or more aggressive than "we" are, it is possible that we subconsciously invoke acts from members of those groups that result more from our own expectations than from the objective characteristics of that group. When you treat somebody else in a friendly way, greeting them and behaving openly, you elicit a different response from the other person than if you treat them distantly or suspiciously, or even try to completely ignore and avoid them.

Immigrants, often called "foreigners," frequently complain that they are treated exclusively as representatives of a group and not as individual people. If a Dutch national commits a crime, then the crime is attributed to that specific individual. The situation is different for ethnic or religious groups. In those cases, the crime, in accordance with the stereotyping, will be described as coming from a Muslim, Mexican, or Iranian. This means that *every* representative of these groups is ascribed a little bit of the blame, not because they have committed the crime, but because they belong to that group. This often results in something we can describe as "double punishment." Members of certain groups already suffer from open or subtle forms of discrimination, and they are punished because *one* member of that group exhibited unacceptable behavior.

To break the pattern of social stereotyping, the cultural anthropologists Toon van Meijl (2020) suggests that we look at people not just as members of a group but also as individual people (see also the various levels of inclusion in Chapter 14). The members of these groups have more *I*-positions or we-positions than just as members of a certain group. They, too, are parents of their children, members of sports clubs, or lovers of a music group. On an individual level, we discern many *I*-positions that offer more levels of contact, understanding, and agreement than what is offered by social stereotypes. Social stereotypes result in more divisions and devaluation than is justified. While social stereotyping often leads to putting up rigid boundaries between groups in society, more open boundaries can arise when we are willing to approach the representatives of these groups also as individual people and human beings.

The conclusion we can draw from this is that democracy can benefit from the lessening of social stereotypes that attach restrictions to the multitude and content of *I*-positions we assign to other people. Democracy, and inner democracy, can benefit from the realistic widening of the number and quality of *I*-positions that are present within ourselves and in other people. If the other person is seen and accepted as "another," then this opens up the opportunity for them to participate in our society from a variety of *I*-positions: Positions that we think are also present in ourselves. In other words, democracy profits from seeing the other as multi-voiced instead of mono-voiced.

Summarizing

- Inner democracy benefits from strengthening our dialogical capability.
- The following factors are essential for this capability: Constructive disagreement with the other, suspension of judgment, and empathy.
- There are different kinds of boundaries between self and other: Soft, rigid, sponge-like, and flexible. Dialogue becomes stimulated through flexible boundaries.
- Democracy at large, and inner democracy, ask for a widening of the position-repertoire that we assign to groups in our society who we consider as "different from us." This stands in stark contrast to the concept of social stereotyping, which invokes rigid boundaries.

Critical Questions

Brown (2006) distinguishes four types of boundary between oneself and another person: soft, rigid, sponge-like, and flexible. Do you feel comfortable with this distinction? Does it give you more insight into various *I*-positions, or does it have any other virtues? And if so, what are they? Or do you think it doesn't add much more to what you already knew?

In the first part of this chapter, we described the boundaries of *I*-positons in relation to another person, or *I*-positions inside yourself. In Chapters (14–16) we moved from personal positions to social (group) positions, and then to collective positions (humanity) and ecological positions (the Earth). What do you think—can you also apply Brown's typology to social, collective, or ecological positions? What would that look like? This is a difficult question, but you can give it a try.

What would Brown's typology mean in regard to the creation of multi-voicedness, as we described in the final paragraph of this chapter? Are there voices within yourself that are barricaded, some you cannot deal with, or voices from which you have closed yourself off?

Exercise

For this exercise you need a group of at least five people, and a maximum of nine. You are going to do a role play, in which four of you are each assigned a role as one of the four boundary types—soft, rigid, sponge-like, and flexible. The fifth person will act as moderator.

The steps are as follows.

- Assign a moderator.
- Choose a discussion topic—something with which all participants can feel involved, something about which they are concerned, or a current very acute and hot topic.

How Can We Promote Inner Democracy? **165**

- The moderator writes down on cards the four position types (soft, rigid, sponge-like, flexible) and gives the cards to the participants in sealed envelopes. So you will know your own position, but nobody else will know it.
- If your group has more than five people, the moderator can distribute second cards with the same positions.
- The moderator takes the initiative by asking a question or formulating a point of view about the topic. Each participant delivers their contributions taking the position described on their card. The moderator ends the discussion after an agreed set time, or when they think there are no more new viewpoints to discover.
- Then you all have a follow-up discussion. At this point, some of the following questions can be discussed:

  a   Did you recognize what positions were taken by the other participants? And how did you notice that?
  b   How did you experience your own position? Was it hard to maintain that position? When was it difficult, and why? What made it easy to do?
  c   What was your experience of communicating with someone who was soft, or sponge-like, or flexible, or rigid? What influence did this have on other participants? What influence did it have on the conversation?
  d   Let everyone think about what they have learned with respect to the topic of discussion. What did you learn? Did you change your opinion on the topic, or not?
  e   Discuss with each other the points above and try to find out what the influence was of the different positions.

Reflecting

- Look at the notes you made under "From Your Own Experience." Compare them with what you have learned from this chapter, and your experiences with Exercise 2. Can you draw some lessons from these comparisons that can strengthen your dialogue skills?
- What, for you, are the most meaningful features described there that might help you with strengthening inner democracy in yourself? Can you describe them in a few short sentences?

18

WHAT OBSTRUCTS OUR INNER DEMOCRACY?

"Good citizenship" requires not only insight into factors that promote inner democracy, but also a feeling for the factors that obstruct it. We will point to three factors that are particularly detrimental to developing inner democracy: Exclusive truth claims, narcissism, and cherishing utopian visions of the future.

From Your Own Experience

Have you recently had a talk with somebody who did not agree with you at all? For example, when you were talking about a certain subject, about what you were thinking, or something you believed in, and then someone else suddenly spoke up and made it clear that you were totally wrong in what you believed. What happened then, how did you experience this? And what did you do, how did you react?

Of course, it often happens that other people have different opinions from you about a certain issue. Sometimes it is not very relevant, or even interesting, to you. But sometimes it can nag at you, or worse. Can you indicate what factors played a role in some examples of how you behaved in those situations? How did you experience this? Try to write this down in a few sentences.

Background Information

Many things in our lives require an opinion. When we encounter a problem, we often come up with an opinion or suggestion that might solve the problem. But as soon as we have formed an opinion and have informed other people about it, we are inclined to stay with that point of view. A lot of people have a hard time changing their opinions. Worse, some people are insensitive to the views of others because they see themselves as the owners of "the truth." We call those people "exclusive truth claimers" who claim, but wrongly so, that there is only *one* truth. If people adhere to this claim, then alternative perspectives are closed off because those people are in the grasp of the "one and only truth." Other opinions are then characterized as "wrong," "inferior," or "nonsense." People who have this outlook on the world close themselves off from what the other person is saying, and they draw rigid boundaries around themselves. If we do this, we cannot learn anything from each other.

Exclusive Truth Claims and Closed Minds

Closing yourself off from other people's points of view and drawing rigid boundaries means having a "closed mind" as opposed to an "open mind." What's the difference? In his book *Principles: Life and work* (2017), US hedge fund manager and philanthropist Ray Dalio describes some of these differences as follows.

- People who put themselves in a closed-minded position do not want to be questioned about their ideas. They get irritated when they notice that other people do not agree with them. In contrast, people who function from within an open-minded attitude get curious if other people do not agree with them. They wonder why the other person is not in agreement with them. They see disagreement as a way to widen their knowledge.
- People who act and think from a closed-minded perspective prefer to get their opinion into the open rather than asking questions. They are not really listening when other people are speaking, but instead they are thinking about how they can defeat the other's viewpoint. But people with an open-minded position take into account that their own point of view might not be the correct one. And that is why they ask questions in order to get corrections.
- People with a closed mind find it difficult to balance two thoughts at the same time. It is only the thought they have at that very moment that determines how they act with regard to other people. People with an open mind can let other people's thoughts influence their own, without relinquishing them. They are able to move between their own thoughts and those of other people.

As these differences indicate, it is not easy to develop an open mind—however, it can be developed through practice and training. Inner democracy is a learning process. That is why we spent time and effort on inner contradiction in Part 1.

Examples of practices for accomplishing an open mind are available in the work of Katy Murphy (2020), who observes that people in close relationships often complain that they do not listen very well to each other. They express this by saying to each other: "You're not listening!" "Let me finish!" "That's not what I said!" Along with the expression "I love you," these complaints are among the most common remarks in close relationships. During her research on listening, she learned something about close relationships that she considered quite ironic: The closer we feel toward another person, the less likely we are to listen carefully to them. This phenomenon is known as the "closeness-communication bias" (Savitsky et al., 2011). It demonstrates that we over-estimate our knowledge about what happens within the mind of the people who are closest to us. We pretend to know what people familiar to us want to express before they actually say something to us. Since we already "know" what is on their mind, we don't need to listen to them and ask questions. Paradoxically, we are inclined to listen better to a stranger than to somebody with whom we have a loving relationship. Apparently, we risk becoming more egocentric as soon as we think we know another person very well.

Narcissism

As people with our own vision of the world, we want our own autonomy to be acknowledged and for other people to take our viewpoint into account. Our position in social relationships gives us a feeling of self-esteem that is conducive to our happiness and well-being. But an over-emphasis on this aspect can lead to narcissism. Self-admiration and wanting to be exceptional can have a really disproportionate effect in some social relations. Researchers Twenge & Campbell (2009) even wrote about a "narcissistic epidemic" in our time. One's own importance can be blown up on the basis of a hidden sense of insecurity. Insecure beautiful women can cultivate their outer appearance with the help of repeated cosmetic-surgery operations; insecure athletes want to reach the top by using performance-enhancing drugs; insecure rich people try to increase their assets with risky loans and hazardous investments; some scientists present enhanced or even false results; idle parents convert their children into a prestigious project that has to come out above other children; and unreal friendships are an artificial product of the explosive spread of social media.

But living in a narcissistically cultivated society doesn't mean that everyone is narcissistic. In an overview article, Vangelisti, Knap, & Daly (1990) describe four features of narcissistic personalities. These characteristics are more prominent in some people than in others.

- *Self-inflation:* People with narcissistic inclinations are overwhelmingly involved with themselves and are influenced by getting admiration from other people. However, their artificially self-inflated self-image is fed by anxiety, vulnerability, and a low level of self-esteem. Narcissistic personalities present themselves from an *I*-position of importance and grandiosity, but underneath there can be found a less conscious, but always present *I*-position of helplessness and futility. Because that position is covered and obscure, it is not easy for these people to engage in a productive dialogue with their weaker aspects and, as a consequence, they do not learn much about themselves.

- *Exploitation*: People who are highly narcissistic try to compensate for their futility and helplessness by looking for power and dominance over others. If other people act on their advice and recommendations, it strengthens a narcissistic personality's vulnerable feeling of self-esteem. But when this doesn't work, they try manipulation and concealment as strategies to make other individuals become subservient to them.
- *Exhibitionism*: Narcissistic personalities keep up a front to the outside world as strong and exceptional figures with a talent to amuse other people and be loved by them. They find it natural to be the center of attention.
- *Impersonal relations*: Narcissists avoid intimate contact and are wary when someone tries to invade their personal space. As a result of not being able to develop intimacy with other people, they often experience feelings of loneliness and are less empathetic towards others.

To find out more about the phenomenon of narcissism, Vangelisti and colleagues (1990) invited subjects to describe the characteristics of people who behave

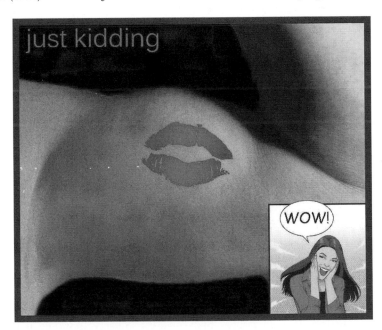

FIGURE 18.1 Body-building arm with an imagined kiss
Source: Wikimedia Commons

170 Part 3 Participation

in a narcissistic way in conversation. They also asked their subjects to imitate the behavior of those people through role-playing. Some interesting characteristics were revealed: Bragging about their own accomplishments, gesturing with hands and other body parts in a demonstrative way, talking in a loud voice, and showing a disinterested facial expression while listening to another person speaking. It turned out that people who were described as narcissistic were considered as less socially appealing. So narcissistic personalities arrive at the exact opposite of their wish to be loved by other people!

To gain insight into narcissism as an obstacle to dialogue, it is important to notice the distinction between "shifting" and "supporting" reactions (Derber, 1979). When someone tells a story, a narcissistic conversation partner is inclined to change the subject and thus direct the attention to themselves. The following example is a good illustration:

DANIEL: "I LIKE MADONNA.":
LISA: "I LIKE BEYONCÉ." (SHIFTING RESPONSE): If Lisa wanted to give a supporting response, she could have asked "Who is your favorite act?" instead of giving her own preference. Responding to the interests of another person requires that conversation partners control their impulse to take over the initiative and postpone their own contribution to the conversation. In this regard, think of the importance of postponing your judgment, a topic we discussed in Part 1.

The flourishing of narcissism in our time asks for an acknowledgement of the fact that we are not only tall, but also small. We started out small and, even when we have grown tall, at the same time, figuratively speaking, we remain small. Tall and small are part of the tension field that stays with us during our entire life. Acknowledging this leads to the experience that we not only admire greatness in other people, and in ourselves, but we also acknowledge the smallness and vulnerability of other people, as well as ourselves, as a precondition for democratic thinking and feeling. Precisely this internal configuration of position (tall) and counter-position (small) is lacking in people who fall prey to self-grandiosity.

The Shadow of Grand Utopias and Ideologies

Freedom and equality are two central pillars of western democracy. The realization of democracy takes place in a tension field—reaching for one value can work at the expense of the other. When people have the complete freedom to organize their lives just as they want, then prosperity for one individual can lead to a conflicting impact on another. However, if they should stay completely equal, that would lead to a curtailment of the freedom that individuals need to fully evolve. This tension field implies that complete equality, just like unlimited freedom, is an illusion. Because both values cannot be fully realized, democracy will always be a thorny path with abysses on both sides. These abysses can only be avoided when democracy is considered not as an existing social reality, but as a permanent learning process of falling and rising, a learning process that never reaches a culmination point. At this juncture we can learn a lot from history.

In the course of history there have always been societal, political, and religious trends which promised that reaching a futuristic utopia can be a realizable goal. This goal functions as an "end position" that can be reached as the present imperfect situation becomes transformed into an eventual perfect one. The assumption is that this end position will free people from the suffering, misery, and failures that overcome them in this "valley of tears." Christianity did this by invoking the image of an afterlife that is only accessible for people who have led virtuous lives. Communism painted vistas of a classless state of freedom in which there is no oppression. Nazism misled people by promising an ideal state in which the Arian race would be lord and master. Neoliberal capitalism announces the salvation message of the free market in which happiness is the result of loans, buying, and selling. In recent decades we have learned about the "doctrine of purity" as preached by some Islamic groups that rely on the original message of the prophet Mohammed. On the basis of such ideals, many generations have been raised in a belief in "pure religion," "superior race," "pure freedom," and even the "blessings of the free market."

Although we can acknowledge that such utopias have instilled purpose and direction in the lives of people who have pursued these ideals, it cannot be denied that their shadow sides have put many people on the wrong track. In Christianity, the divide between heaven and hell, between exclusive good and

FIGURE 18.2 The seductive power of grandiose utopias
Source: Wikimedia Commons

evil, and between gods and idols has led to rampant religious wars and the extermination of "heretics" who hold "the wrong view." Communism resulted in terror and mass executions during Stalin's regime in Russia and Mao Tse Tung's command in China. Nazism led to the horrific Holocaust with its mass executions, concentration camps, and gas chambers. Neoliberalism has contributed to the worldwide exploitation of indigenous groups and the continuous depletion of natural resources. Ultra-orthodox ideas in certain Islamic groups are put to the service of political extremism and terrorism, or have created these.

What are the implications of these criticisms for a democratic society? Current societies, in which people and groups in the population are more than ever connected to and dependent upon each other, don't ask for utopias based on illusions, but look for the acknowledgement of realistic tension fields between various religious movements, between people with different skin colors, between free and guided forms of economy, and between economy and ecology. Instead of going after the exclusive correctness of one's own utopia, a democratic movement asks for change through debate and dialogue between people who hold different viewpoints. This implies a recognition of democracy as a continuous process of positioning and counter-positioning in which social differences do not necessarily have to lead to unworkable polarization, but can be challenged and complement each other as part of a never-ending process of searching. In the end it is a continuous process of positioning and counter-positioning that takes place not in a linear way towards an ideal and a predictable end-point, but as a non-linear, searching quest in the direction of a rather unknown future.

What does this mean for the development of the individual self? An exclusive utopian ideal promoted by an individual or group has two implications. First, rejecting another, rival utopia can result in closing off the boundaries of the self in a rigid way and becoming blind to alternative positions. Furthermore, such a position-repertoire shows a strong hierarchical order in which many positions get subordinated to the top position that fuels the utopia. The I-positions that are subordinated to the top position, can then no longer be shared with other people who hold different world views. Think, for example, about the restrictions that an orthodox religious doctrine places on the development of specific I-positions in their position-repertoire (e.g., one's attitude to food, sex, marriage, or child-rearing). Another example is the case of excessive consumerism in a market economy, where we see many I-positions come under the influence of "I as a consumer" as the dominant position in the organization of the self (e.g., buying sex, consuming information, paying for instant happiness). Inner democracy becomes obstructed when one of the I-positions in your inner self gains a structural power position and, as a consequence, the voices of opposing or alternative positions have to succumb to this overpowering I-position.

Summarizing

- Inner democracy can become blocked by exclusive truth-claims. This is frequently accompanied by a "closed mind" with rigid boundaries between yourself and the other person, so that the self closes itself off from alternative viewpoints.
- Inner democracy can also become obstructed by a narcissistic attitude that is characterized by self-inflation, exploitation of other people, exhibitionism, and impersonal relationships, along with neglect or suppression of one's weaker *I*-positions.
- In addition, utopian thinking has an obstructive influence on inner democracy. The boundaries between oneself and the disagreeing other person get closed off in a rigid way. The position-repertoire becomes organized in a rigid and hierarchical way, with the result that many other *I*-positions become subordinated to it.

Critical Questions

In the text we refer to the book *Principles* by Ray Dalio, who makes a distinction between an "open mind" and a "closed mind." If we understand Dalio correctly, then we can all develop an open mind if we want to, and if we make an effort to reach it. Do you think this is possible? Can we learn to accomplish this? Or is having an open or closed mind something that is already a given, something innate, from birth? Or maybe it is something that has developed over time subconsciously and we can no longer change it?

If an open mind has so many preferable characteristics compared to a closed mind, why do we still come across people who have a closed mind? Are there sometimes advantages to closing off your own mind?

Twenge and Campbell argue that we live in a society that cultivates narcissism. This means, according to them, that we live in a society where many of us emphasize our own important ego. What phenomena do you see around you that strengthen this position? And what do you see around you that undermines this argument?

The third theme of this chapter describes the danger of grand utopias. As examples we mentioned Nazism, communism under Stalin and Mao, ultra-orthodoxies in Christianity and Islam, and neoliberalism. These all differ vastly in scope. Do you think it is correct to place them under one denominator? Do they all carry an element of danger?

174   Part 3 Participation

Exercises

Exercise 1

Closing yourself off from the opinions of other people and drawing rigid boundaries involves, according to Ray Dalio, the distinction between an "open mind" and a "closed mind." People with an "open mind":

- become curious when other people don't agree with them
- are curious about (critical) questions regarding their own opinions
- are capable of moving back and forth between various different thoughts.

This is what we are going to practice. Write down a statement, something you feel very certain about, and preferably something you also feel passionate about.

I believe that ...

From which *I*-position did you write down this statement? ("I as a student," or "I as a commuter," or "I as ... "). Give some arguments:

I as [A] think that ...
  because ...
  because ...
  because ...

By now you have learned that there are many individuals who hold very different opinions about certain topics. Do you have any idea who those individuals might be? Write down a contrary *I*-position according to an individual who holds a different point of view, putting yourself in their shoes:

I as ...

(To help you out a bit: If you formulate an opinion from the standpoint of "I as a student" you can probably imagine that a teacher or school management person thinks differently about the same subject.)

Now formulate another opinion coming from the contrary position (e.g., from a teacher, or from a management position):

I as [B] think that ...
  because ...
  because ...
  because ...

Now try to move back and forth, as if commuting between these two opinions. Try not to just formulate arguments that are opposite to each other. It's much better to let your *I*-positions ask questions of each other:

What exactly do you mean by … ?
What are your grounds for that argument … ?
Why do you think … is a good argument?
What could be the result of this?
etc.

Try again to go back and forth between the *I*-positions (your own, A and the other one, B). Ask a couple of questions from your own position (with answers of course), and a couple of questions from the other position. This way a meta-dialogue can arise in which you slowly but surely investigate wether your original thoughts are valid, or have changed—this often happens, but not always. However, you will have learned something new and developed a better or more nuanced foundation for your own opinions.

Exercise 2

By now, you know a lot about all kinds of mechanisms, attitudes, and arguments in communications among people that can help you understand how to promote inner democracy, use of contradictory arguments, and learn from and with each other, and how elements can work in a constructive or obstructive way.

A video on YouTube portrays a conversation between a nurse and a patient: https://youtu.be/W1RY_72O_LQ

Much goes wrong in this conversation. Watch the video (it lasts about 4 minutes) and make notes on which of these problematic practices you can recognize:

- soft boundaries
- rigid boundaries
- sponge-like boundaries
- ascribing a stereotype to another person
- self-inflation
- exploitation
- exhibitionism
- being impersonal.

Of course, both people in the video don't get everything wrong (or do they?) At what moments in the conversation can you observe these good practices:

- flexible boundaries
- open dialogue
- active listening
- empathy
- asking open questions

- paraphrasing or summarizing what the other is saying.

The nurse and patient reinforce each other's attitude in their conversation. Suppose you were one of the two participants in this conversation, and you want to put yourself in a dialogical position towards the other person, who is not doing so. How would you handle this?

Reflecting

- Do many people think you are a democrat? And can they also identify you as a person who is a democrat within their inner self? Probably nobody will respond 100 percent "yes" to the second question. Why? Or why not?
- What kind of obstructive factors can you detect in yourself? What has specifically stimulated inner democracy in you?
- Place those stimulating and obstructive factors within yourself on a pair of scales. Which side does the scale tilt to?

What is the relationship between the scale's positions and your various *I*-positions? In other words: Are there *I*-positions in which the promoting factors are stronger, or in which the obstructing factors are stronger? How can you use this in a meta-conversation between your *I*-positions? How can you, or how would you like to, apply what you have already learned about your inner democracy?

Now go back to what you said under "From Your Own Experience." Did the text and exercises have some influence on you? Has anything changed? If the points you mentioned there have not changed, why is that?

FIGURE 18.3 Scale of justice
Source: Wikimedia Commons

EPILOGUE TO PART 3

Democracy cannot exist without you, or without us—we have to work together on this. Democracy always involves multiple people, on a smaller scale in a family or a classroom, or on a wider scale—a country, a continent, or all of us together, including our ecological environment. The starting point of this book is the thesis that people are not independent of each other, we do not exist in our own bubble, but we are all part of something that is larger than us. Other people are even within you, they contribute to the constellation of who you are. The other, or others, in our selves function as I-positions.

In a democracy, it is vital that we work together. That requires that we open ourselves up to other people, to admit opposition and to enter into a dialogue with other people, even if they disagree with us. But when those other individuals are also represented in ourselves, then we can admit this opposition also in ourselves, and use it for the development of meaningful relations with others and ourselves. We can thus also entertain a dialogue in our inner self, between our own I-positions, even when they conflict with each other. So this is our proposal: Start within yourself, with your inner democracy. Not as a replacement for democracy at large, but as an exercise and development of your own democratic capability and attitude: Democracy starts within yourself!

Democracy never stops; as the American philosopher and pedagogue John Dewey (1938) argued, it has to be *invented* continually and shaped by current living generations. Democracy is a continuous process of debate and dialogue, also within yourself.

178 Part 3 Participation

Self-Quiz for Part 3

To strengthen your memory storage of what you have learned so far, at the end of each Part you will find a self-quiz consisting of 10 multiple-choice questions to check if you have correctly digested the background information. To pass the quiz, you need to give at least 7 correct answers to the 10 questions. If you do not pass the test, you are invited to re-examine the chapters of that Part and answer the quiz questions again. The correct answers are included in the Appendix at the end of the book. This method ensures that you get specific feedback about the level of your knowledge regarding a certain topic, and that you have mastered the content of the chapters.

Each question has four alternative answers. For each question there is only one correct or best answer. Select just one answer to each question.

1. Which of the *I*-positions mentioned below can be considered as someone's social identity?

   a I the dreamer
   b I the homosexual
   c I the human being
   d I the caring person

2. What is the meaning of the paradigm of the minimal group? It means that:

   a a group doesn't necessarily have to be big to give you the feeling that you are part of it
   b a little difference alone can give rise to a group
   c people with minimal differences in their own group can equate themselves with another sub-group
   d minimally we consider ourselves always as part of a group

3. According to research, what is the important advantage when we move from "me as a member of a group" to "me as a human being"? We can:

   a better develop our identity
   b become more forgiving
   c improve our leadership qualities
   d have fewer prejudices

4. What responsibility belongs to the *I*-position "I as a human being"? The responsibility for:

   a myself
   b my family, friends, etc.
   c all people on Earth
   d the Earth

Epilogue to Part 3   **179**

5. What is the most important characteristic of someone with sponge-like boundaries? They are a person who:

   a   incorporates everything without making preferences
   b   cannot assert their independence very well
   c   always emulates the behavior and the ideas of other people
   d   never keeps an appointment

6. What is important in using flexible boundaries? You can:

   a   deal with every situation
   b   alternate between being open and closed to the opinions of other people
   c   know very well what your opinion is
   d   take into account the opinions of other people

7. What is a stereotype?

   a   a judgment that cannot be changed
   b   an opinion about a certain group of people
   c   an attribute that is allocated to an entire part of the population
   d   a characteristic of a group or individual with inadequate foundation

8. Empathy is a pre-requisite for starting a dialogue. Which of the statements below do *not* imply empathy?

   a   the capacity to identify yourself in a cognitive way with the points of view of another person
   b   the capacity to identify yourself in an emotional way with the feelings of another person
   c   showing forgiveness regarding the acts of another person
   d   feeling compassion for another person

9. Narcissism is a strongly obstructive factor for achieving inner democracy. What are the four characteristics of a narcissistic personality?

   a   self-inflation, disdain of other people, exhibitionism, not capable of entertaining personal relations
   b   self-inflation, disdain of other people, only capable of forming a group-identity, not capable of forming personal relationships
   c   self-inflation, exploitation of other people, exhibitionism, not being able to engage in personal relationships
   d   positive self-image, exploitation of other people, only capable of forming a group identity, not capable of engaging in personal relationships

180 Part 3 Participation

10. What is the reason that utopian thinking has an obstructive influence on reaching inner democracy?

    a   Someone who thinks in a utopian way thinks only about the *I*-positon: "I as a part of the Earth"

    b   Someone who thinks in a utopian way has organized their position-repertoire in a firmly hierarchical way

    c   Someone who thinks in a utopian way does not pay much attention to their own identity

    d   Someone who thinks in a utopian way is not emphatic

REFERENCES

Alemanno, A. (2020). Taming COVID-19 by regulation: An opportunity for self-reflection. *European Journal of Risk Regulation*, April 24, 1–8.

Amnesty International (2016). *"This is what we die for": Human rights abuses in the Democratic Republic of the Congo power the global trade in cobalt.* London: Amnesty International.

Aron, A., Mashek, D., McLaughlin-Volpe, T., Wright, S., Lewandowski, G., & Aron, E. (2005). Including close others in the cognitive structure of the self. In M. Baldwin (ed.), *Interpersonal cognition* (pp. 206–232). New York: Guilford Press.

Arora, S., Rajwade, J.M., & Paknikar, K.M. (2012) Nanotoxicology and in vitro studies: The need of the hour. *Toxicology and Applied Pharmacology*, 258, 151–165.

Bahl, S. (2012). Navigating inconsistent consumption preferences at multiple levels of the dialogical self. In H.J.M. Hermans & T. Gieser (eds), *Handbook of Dialogical Self Theory* (pp. 470–487). Cambridge, UK: Cambridge University Press.

Barber, B.R. (2006). Consumed: The fate of citizens under capitalism triumphant. Three lectures for the Shih Ming Teh lectureship, Taipei, December. https://ce399resist.files.wordpress.com/2012/02/barbers-3-lectures.pdf

Barragan, R.C., Brooks, R., & Meltzoff, A.N. (2020). Altruistic food sharing behavior by human infants after a hunger manipulation. *Science Reports*, 10, 1785.

Biesta, G.J.J. (2016). *Beyond learning: Democratic education for a human future.* New York: Routledge.

Bohm, D. (1996). *On dialogue.* New York: Routledge.

Bohm, D., Factor, D., & Garrett, P. (1991). Dialogue: A proposal. *Infed*, http://www.infed.org/archives/e-texts/bohm_dialogue.htm

Bouie, J. (2020). Why coronavirus is killing African-Americans more than others: Higher rates of infection and death among minorities demonstrate the racial character of inequality in America. *The New York Times*, April 14.

Boykoff, M., Goodman, M., & Littler, J. (2010). 'Charismatic megafauna': The growing power of celebrities and pop culture in climate change campaigns. Environment, Politics and

182 References

Development Working Paper Series No. 28. London: Kings College London. http://centaur.reading.ac.uk/56262/

Braman, D., Kahan, D.M., Slovic, P., Gastil, J., & Cohen, G.L. (2007). Affect, values, and nanotechnology risk perceptions: An experimental investigation. *GW Law Faculty Publications & Other Works*, 207. https://scholarship.law.gwu.edu/faculty_publications/207

Bray, J., Johns, N., & Kilburn, D. (2011) An exploratory study into the factors impeding ethical consumption. *Journal of Business Ethics*, 98, 597–608.

Bremmers, C. (2019) *Interesse en nabijheid. Interview tijdens symposium Ecologisch bevraagd, pedagogisch uitgedaagd*. Amsterdam: Gezelschap Waardenwerk [Society Value Work], 15 maart.

Brinthaupt, T.M. & Dove, C.T. (2012). Differences in self-talk frequency as a function of age, only-child, and imaginary childhood companion status. *Journal of Research in Personality*, 46, 326–333.

Brown, N.W. (2006). *Coping with infuriating, mean, critical people: The destructive narcissistic pattern*. Westport, CT: Praeger.

Brown, R.A., Lejuez, C.W., Kahler, C.W., & Strong, D.R. (2002). Distress tolerance and duration of past smoking cessation attempts. *Journal of Abnormal Psychology*, 111, 180–185.

Burgoon, J.K., & Jones, S.B. (1976). Toward a theory of personal space expectations and their violations. *Human Communication Research*, 2, 131–146.

Burson, M.C. (2002). Finding clarity in the midst of conflict: Facilitating dialogue and skillful discussion using a model from the Quaker tradition. *Group Facilitation: A Research and Applications Journal*, 4, 23–29.

Caprara, G.V. & Vecchione, M. (2017). *Personalizing politics and realizing democracy*. New York: Oxford University Press.

Carlson, S.M. & Moses, L.J. (2001). Individual differences in inhibitory control and children's theory of mind. *Child Development*, 72, 1032–1053.

Caves, R.W. (2004). *Encyclopedia of the city*. New York: Routledge, p. 97.

Cowe, R. & Williams, S. (2000). *Who are the ethical consumers?* Ethical Consumerism Report. London: Cooperative Bank.

Dalio, R. (2017). *Principles: Life and work*. New York: Simon & Schuster.

Damasio, A.R. (1994). *Descartes' error: Emotion, reason, and the human brain*. New York: Putnam Publishing.

De Bono, E. (1985). *Six thinking hats: An essential approach to business management*. London: Little, Brown.

Decety, J. & Jackson, P.L. (2004). The functional architecture of human empathy. *Behavioral and Cognitive Neuroscience Reviews*, 3, 71–100.

Dehaene, S. & Naccache, L. (2001) Towards a cognitive neuroscience of consciousness: basic evidence and a workspace framework. *Cognition*, 79, 1–37.

Derber, C. (1979). *The pursuit of attention: Power and individualism in everyday life*. Boston, MA: G.K. Hall.

Dewey, J. (1910). *How we think*. Lexington, DC: Heath & Co.

Dewey, J. (1938). *Experience and education*. New York: Kappa Delta Phi.

Dex, S., Willis, J., Paterson. R., & Sheppard, E. (2000). Freelance workers and contract uncertainty: The effects of contractual changes in the television industry. *Work Employment & Society*, 14, 283–305.

Edwards, D. & Jacobs, M. (2003). *Conscious and unconscious*. Maidenhead, UK: Open University Press/McGraw-Hill Education.

References 183

Elbow, P. (1973). *Writing without teachers*. New York: Oxford University Press.

Elliott, R., Bohart, A.C., Watson, J.C., & Greenberg, L.S. (2011). Empathy. In J. Norcross (ed.), *Psychotherapy relationships that work*, 2nd edn (pp. 132–152). New York: Oxford University Press.

Fecho, B. (2004). *Is this English? Race, language, and culture in the class-room*. New York: Teachers College Press.

Feshbach, N.D. & Feshbach, S. (2009). Empathy and education. In J. Decety & W. Ickes (eds), *The social neuroscience of empathy* (pp. 85–97). Cambridge, MA: MIT Press.

Friedman, T.L. (1999). *The Lexus and the olive tree*. New York: Farrar, Straus and Giroux.

Gastil, J. (1994). A definition and illustration of democratic leadership. *Human Relations*, 47, 953–975.

Gerstadt, C.L., Hong, Y.J., & Diamond, A. (1994). The relationship between cognition and action: Performance of children 3.5–7 years old on a Stroop-like day–night test. *Cognition*, 53, 129–153.

Goleman, D. (2007). Three kinds of empathy: Cognitive, emotional, compassionate. Online post, June 12. http://www.danielgoleman.info/three-kinds-of-empathy-cogniti ve-emotional-compassionate/

Grossman, I. & Kross, E. (2014). Exploring Solomon's paradox: Self-distancing eliminates the self-other asymmetry in wise reasoning about close relationships in younger and older adults. *Psychological Science*, 25, 1571–1580.

Haidt, J., Rosenberg, E., & Hom, H. (2003). Differentiating diversities: Moral diversity is not like other kinds. *Journal of Applied Social Psychology*, 33, 1–36.

Heijne, B. (2017). Het radicale antwoord op haat is waardigheid, *NRC*, 9 September.

Hermans, H.J.M. (2018). *Society in the self: A theory of identity in democracy*. New York: Oxford University Press.

Hermans, H.J.M. (2020). *Inner democracy: Empowering the mind against a polarizing society*. New York: Oxford University Press.

Hermans, H.J.M. & Hermans-Konopka, A. (2010). *Positioning and counter-positioning in a globalizing society*. Cambridge, UK: Cambridge University Press.

Horowitz, A. (2013). *On looking. Eleven walks with expert eyes*. New York: Scribner.

Hyde, B. & Bineham, J.L. (2000). From debate to dialogue: Toward a pedagogy of non-polarized public discourse. *Southern Communication Journal*, 65, 208–223.

Isakhan, B. (2012). Introduction: The complex and contested history of democracy. In B. Isakhan & S. Stockwell (eds), *The Edinburgh companion to the history of democracy* (pp. 1–25). Edinburgh, UK: Edinburgh University Press.

Itzchakov, G., Kluger, A.N., & Castro, D.R. (2017). I am aware of my inconsistencies but can tolerate them: The effect of high quality listening on speakers' attitude ambivalence. *Personality and Social Psychology Bulletin*, 43, 105–120.

James, W. (1890). *The Principles of Psychology*. New York: Holt.

Johnson, L. & Morris, P. (2010). Towards a framework for critical citizenship education. *Curriculum Journal*, 21, 77–96.

Kang, S.H.K. (2016). Spaced repetition promotes efficient and effective learning: Policy implications for instruction. *Policy Insights from the Behavioral and Brain Sciences*, 3, 12–19.

Kassem, C.L. (2000). Implementation of a school-wide approach to critical thinking instruction. *American Secondary Education*, 29, 26–36.

Kenen, R.H. (1984). Making agreements with oneself: Prelude to social behavior. *Sociological Forum*, 1, 362–377.

184 References

Kent, D. (2019). *The countries where people are most dissatisfied with how democracy is working.* Washington, DC: Pew Research Center.

Kessels, J., Boers, E., & Mostert, P. (2002). *Vrije ruimte.* Amsterdam: Boom.

Kimmel, M.S., & Mahler, M. (2003). Adolescent masculinity, homophobia, and violence: Random school shootings, 1982–2001. *American Behavioral Scientist, 46,* 1439–1458.

Kolb, D. A. (1984). *Experiential learning: Experience as the source of learning and development.* Englewood Cliffs, NJ: Prentice-Hall.

Konopka, A. & van Beers, W. (2014). Composition work: A method for self-investigation. *Journal of Constructivist Psychology, 27,* 194–210.

Kreijns, K., Kirschner, P.A., Jochems, W., & van Buuren, H. (2004). Determining sociability, social space, and social presence in (A)synchronous collaborative groups. *Cyberpsychology & Behavior, 7,* 155–172.

Kross, E., Ayduk, O., & Mischel, W. (2005). When asking "Why" does not hurt: Distinguishing rumination from reflective processing of negative emotions. *Psychological Science, 9,* 709–715.

Kuitenbrouwer, J. (2014). Dialoog: eerst het eten and dan de moraal [Dialogue: First the food and then the morals].*NRC,* 16 January.

LeDoux, J. (2002). *Synaptic self: How our brains become who we are.* New York: Penguin Viking.

Lehmann, O.V., Kardum, G., & Klempe, S.H. (2019). The search for inner-silence as a source for *Eudaimonia. British Journal of Guidance & Counselling, 47,* 180–189.

Lengelle, R., (2016). What a career coach can learn from a playwrite: Expressive dialogues for identity development. In H.J.M. Hermans (ed.). *Assessing and stimulating a dialogical self in groups, teams, cultures, and organizations* (pp. 37–53). New York: Springer.

Lewis, M.D. (2002). The dialogical brain: Contributions of emotional neurobiology to understanding the dialogical self. *Theory & Psychology, 12,* 175–190.

Lovell, G. (2000). *Consultancy, ministry and mission: A handbook for practitioner and work consultants in Christian organizations.* Warsaw: Burns and Oates.

Ma-Kellams, C. & Blascovich, J. (2012). Inferring the emotions of friends versus strangers: The role of culture and self-construal. *Personality and Social Psychology Bulletin, 38,* 933–945.

MacMath, S. (2008). Implementing a democratic pedagogy in the classroom: Putting Dewey into practice. *Canadian Journal for New Scholars in Education, 1,* 1–12.

Marková, I. (1987). On the interaction of opposites in psychological processes. *Journal for the Theory of Social Behaviour, 17,* 279–299.

McGregor, I. & Marigold, D. C. (2003). Defensive zeal and the uncertain self: What makes you so sure? *Journal of Personality and Social Psychology, 85,* 838–852.

McGregor, S. (1999). Towards a rationale for integrating consumer and citizenship education. *Journal of Consumer Studies & Home Economics, 23,* 207–211.

Meadows, D.H., Meadows, D.L., Randers, J., & Behrens, W.W. (1972) *The limits to growth: A report for the Club of Rome's project on the predicament of mankind.* New York: Universe Books.

van Meijl, T. (2020). Dialog for de-radicalization in postcolonial Europe. *Journal of Constructivist Psychology, 33,* 235–247.

Mersch, R. (2016). *Waarom iedereen altijd gelijk heeft [Why everybody is always right].* Amsterdam: De Bezige Bij.

Monereo, C. (2019). The role of critical incidents in the dialogical construction of teacher identity. Analysis of a professional transition case. *Learning, Culture and Social Interaction*, 20, 4–13.

Morris, B.J. (2018). *The feminist revolution. The struggle for women's liberation*. Washington, DC: Smithsonian Books.

Murphy, K. (2020). You're not listening. Here's why. *The New York Times*, February 11. https://www.nytimes.com/2020/02/11/well/family/listening-relationships-marria ge-closeness-communication-bias.html

Nederveen, P. (2019) We zijn een nieuwe moral aan het uitvinden [We are discovering a new morality]. Interview. *NRC*, October 16.

Oreskes, N. & Conway, E.M. (2014). *The collapse of western civilization: A view from the future*. New York: Columbia University Press.

Pakaluk, M. (2005). *Aristotle's Nicomachean ethics: An introduction*. Cambridge, UK: Cambridge University Press.

Peffley, M. & Rohrschneider, R. (2003). Democratization and political tolerance in seventeen countries: A multi-level model of democratic learning. *Political Research Quarterly*, 56, 243–257.

Pelling, M. (2011). *Adaptation to climate change: From resilience to transformation*. London: Routledge.

Rachman, G. (2019). High stakes in Hong Kong: Xi's great challenge. *Financial Times*, November 27.

Rezabakhsh, B., Bornemann, D., Hansen, U., & Schrader, U. (2006). Consumer power: A comparison of the old economy and the internet economy. *Journal of Consumer Policy*, 29, 3–36.

Rogers, C. (1951). *Client-centered therapy: Its current practice, implications and theory*. Boston, MA: Houghton Mifflin.

Roth-Hanania, R., Bush-Rossnagel, N., & Higgins-D'Alessandro, A. (2000). Development of self and empathy in early infancy: Implications for atypical development. *Infants & Young Children*, 13, 1–14.

Sampson, H. (2020). You want to be a responsible tourist. But what does that even mean? *The Washington Post*, January 16.

Savitsky, K., Keysar, B., Epley, N., Carter, T., & Swanson, A. (2011). The closeness-communication bias: Increased egocentrism among friends versus strangers. *Journal of Experimental Social Psychology*, 47, 269–273.

Schulz, W., Ainley, J., Fraillon, J., Losito, B., Agrusti, G., & Friedman, T. (2018). *Becoming Citizens in a changing world. IEA International Civic and Citizenship Education Study 2016: International report*. Open access publication, https://www.springer.com/gp/book/9783319739625

Shah, S. (2016). *Pandemic: Tracking contagions, from cholera to Ebola and beyond*. New York: Macmillan.

Simons, D.J. & Chabris, C.F. (1999). Gorillas in our midst: Sustained inattentional blindness for dynamic events. *Perception*, 28, 1059–1074.

Snyder, M., Tanke, E.D., & Berscheid, E. (1977). Social perception and interpersonal behavior: On the self-fulfilling nature of social stereotypes. *Journal of Personality and Social Psychology*, 35, 656–666.

Somers, M. (2020). We hebben een vaccin nodig. Maar vooral politieke wil [We need a vaccine. However, above all, political will]. Interview with Sonia Shah. *NRC*, June 9.

186 References

Sommer, F., Leuschner, V., & Scheithauer, H. (2014). Bullying, romantic rejection, and conflicts with teachers: The crucial role of social dynamics in the development of school shootings. A systematic review. *International Journal of Developmental Science*, 8, 3–24.

Tajfel, H. & Turner, J. C. (1979). An integrative theory of intergroup conflict. In W.G. Austin & S. Worchel (eds), *The social psychology of intergroup relations* (pp. 33–47). Monterey, CA: Brooks-Cole.

Thomassen, J., Van Ham, C., & Andeweg, R. (2014). *De wankele democratie: Heeft de democratie haar beste tijd gehad?*Amsterdam: Prometheus-Bert Bakker.

Tuller, H.M., Bryan, C.J., Heyman, G.D., & Christenfeld, N.J.S. (2015). Seeing the other side: Perspective taking and the moderation of extremity. *Journal of Experimental Social Psychology*, 59, 18–23.

Turner, J.C., Hogg, M.A., Oakes, P.J., Reicher, S.D., & Wetherell, M.S. (1987). *Rediscovering the social group: A self-categorization theory*. Oxford, UK: Basil Blackwell.

Twenge, J.M., & Campbell, W.K. (2009). *The Narcissism Epidemic: Living in the age of entitlement*. New York: Free Press.

Van der Staak, C. (2011). Ambivalent verlangen. *Maandblad voor Geestelijke Volksgezondheid* [*Monthly Journal for Mental Health*], 66, 74–78.

Vangelisti, A.L., Knapp, M.L., & Daly, J.A. (1990). Conversational narcissism. *Communication Monographs*, 57, 251–274.

Weishar, J. (2018). The truth about people who "compartmentalize." *Lifestyle*, February 4.

Whelton, W.J. (2001). Emotion in self-criticism. PhD thesis, York University, Toronto, Canada.

Wohl, M.J.A. & Branscombe, N.R. (2005). Forgiveness and collective guilt assignment to historical perpetrator groups depend on level of social category inclusiveness. *Journal of Personality and Social Psychology*, 88, 288–303.

APPENDIX

Correct answers to the self quizzes

Correct answer at Part 1 Opposition

1. a
2. b
3. c
4. a
5. b
6. d
7. b
8. c
9. d
10. b

Correct answers at Part 2 Cooperation

1. a
2. a
3. c
4. b
5. d
6. a
7. a
8. c
9. b
10. c

Correct answers at Part 3 Participation

1. b
2. b
3. b
4. c
5. b
6. b
7. c
8. c
9. c
10. b

INDEX

abortion 89, 90–91, 97
accountability 97
active listening 80–84, 125, 126, 175
addiction 5–6, 37, 42, 160
African Americans 47, 143–144
agreements with yourself 69–70, 71, 74, 75–76
Alemanno, A. xxi
alter-ego 8, 111
alternative points of view xvii–xviii, 11–18, 48, 49, 62, 89, 166–167; *see also* opinions
ambivalence 81–82, 83
amygdala 55
Andeweg, R. 58
anger 37, 38–39, 53, 55
anxiety 37, 53, 65, 160
arguments 79–80, 107
Aristotle 8
Aron, A. 98
attention 20–21, 56, 59

Bahl, Shalini 34
Barragan, R.C. 124n1
Bineham, J.L. 108, 109
body language 4, 21, 22, 111
Bohm, David 20, 21, 64
boomerang effect 80
Bouie, J. 143–144
boundaries 14–16, 48, 63, 164–165, 179; crossing 98, 109, 132; exclusive truth claims 167; in-groups and out-groups 47, 49, 99, 100, 102; moral opinions

127; opening and closing 155, 157–162; social stereotypes 163, 164
Boykoff, M. 148–149
brain circuits 55–56
Branscombe, N.R. 140
Bray, J. 45, 46
Bremmers, Chris 153
Brooks, R. 124n1
Brown, Nina 14, 158, 164
bubbles 11, 13, 16, 29, 98, 109
Burgoon, J.K. 158

Campbell, W.K. 168, 173
capitalism 171
Carlson, S.M. 116
Castro, D.R. 80–82
changing perspective 25–31, 48, 49, 108
children 115–117, 124n1, 158
China 14–15
Christianity 171–172, 173
citizenship: consumer-citizens 35, 43–44, 46, 149; definition of xx; global xvii, 142; multilevel xx–xxi; personal xvi
Civic and Citizenship Education (CCE) xxiv
civil rights xv, 58
climate change xx, 17, 132, 147; depolarization 101; fairness and justice 150–151; moral positions 89, 91; music and pop culture 148–149
close relationships 98, 167–168
closed minds 92, 167, 173, 174

190 Index

closed positions 15, 17, 21, 37, 50, 63, 98, 155
coalitions xviii
cognitive empathy 116–117, 118, 122, 123, 125, 179
collaboration xxi–xxii
collective identity 132; *see also* human identity
collective responsibility xx, xxiv, 151
commonality 111, 143, 144
communism 171, 172, 173
compartmentalization 58–59
compassion 117, 119–120, 122, 125, 179
Composition Method 61n1
conflict 4, 96
confusion 54, 81, 159
constructive criticism of yourself 70, 73–74, 75, 77
consulting yourself 70, 71–73, 74, 75, 76–77, 126
consumer-citizens 35, 43–44, 46, 149
consumerism 172
consumption behavior 34–36, 37, 44–46
contradiction 29, 58, 59, 82–83; *see also* inner contradiction; opposition
Conway, E.M. 132
cooperation xvii, xviii, xxii, 107
coronavirus pandemic xx–xxi, 42, 143–144, 149–150
counter-arguments 79–80, 83
counter-positioning 4, 5–6, 8, 9; changing perspective 27; democracy as process of 172; emotion and reason 53, 58; inner contradiction 50; uncertainty 43
Cowe, R. 44–45
critical thinking xiv, xxii, 73
criticism of self 70, 73–74, 75, 77, 126
cultural diversity 89, 90
cynicism 46

Dalio, Ray 167, 173, 174
Daly, J.A. 168–170
debate 105–107, 111–112, 127, 172, 177
decision making 39, 44, 54, 160
defensiveness 80, 83, 109, 156–157
Dehaene, S. 56
deliberation 35
deliberative climate 101
democracy xiv–xv, 5, 177; contradiction 82; external and internal xxi, xxv; freedom and equality 170; illiberal democracies 61n2; as learning process 170–171; multiple *I*-positions 163;

opposition xvii, 29, 62, 125; political tolerance 56–58; transformative dialogue xxii; *see also* inner democracy
democratic attitude xv–xvi, 121, 177
Democrats 88
demographic diversity 90
depolarization 82, 83, 94–104, 125, 127
depression 42, 73
Descartes, R. 53
Dewey, John xxi, xxii, 73, 177
Dex, S. 43
dialogue xvi, 20, 62, 105–114, 126, 127; democracy 172, 177; dialogical capability 161–162, 164; emotion and reason 53, 58–59; empathy 157, 179; inner democracy 155–156; open 14, 175; transformative xxii; *see also* inner dialogue
Diamond, A. 117
disagreement 4, 109, 156, 164, 167; *see also* contradiction; opposition
discrimination 47, 141, 142–143, 144, 163
distancing 36, 37–39, 72
diversity 89, 90
drawing 120–121, 122

Earth xx, 132, 133, 147–154
echo chambers 11, 13, 29
ecological awareness xiv, 148
ecological identity xiv, 132, 147–154
ecological responsibility xx, xxiv, 44, 151–152
Edwards, D. 56
egalitarian attitude 88, 100–101
ego 8, 173
Ekman, Paul 118, 119
elections xv, 56, 105, 106
emotional empathy 116, 119, 122, 123, 125, 179
emotions xvi, 23, 52–61, 63, 88–89; attention to emotional responses 20–21; dialogical capability 161–162; inner dialogue xviii; meta-positions 37–39; moral issues 91, 92–93, 125; suspension of judgment 64; uncertainty 41–42
empathy 14, 83, 115–124, 125, 128, 175; changing perspective 26, 29; dialogue 157, 164, 179; empathy training 96; lack of 91; social identity 134–135
environment xiv, 153; *see also* ecological identity
ethical purchasing 44–46
exclusive truth claims 166–167, 173

exhibitionism 169, 173, 175, 179
experts 100–102
exploitation 169, 173, 175, 179

fairness 150–151
Fatboy Slim 148
Feshbach, Norma and Seymour 120–121
flame wars 13, 18n2
flexibility 43, 62, 155; boundaries 15–16, 159–160, 161, 162, 164–165, 175, 179; changing perspective 25–31, 48, 49, 108; levels of inclusion 150
forgiveness 140
freedom 170, 171
freedom of speech xv, 56
friendship 8, 99
future planning 37

Gandhi, Mahatma 141–142, 145
gay rights 89, 90–91
gender equality 89–90
Gerstadt, C.L. 117
global citizenship xvii, 142
Global Cool 149
globalization 42, 109
Goleman, Daniel 118, 119
Goodman, M. 148–149
grand utopias 171–172
groups: boundaries 47, 48, 49; citizens 149; empathy 121; group cultures 13; groupthink 13; identity xx, 99, 125, 131, 132, 133–138, 140, 142–143; opposition 94, 98–102; prejudice/discrimination against 142–143, 145; social responsibility 151; social stereotypes 162–163
guilt 54, 65

Haidt, J. 90
Heijne, Bas 141
helicopter view 33–34, 37, 39, 48, 49, 63
help, giving and receiving 4, 5, 119
Hermans, H.J.M. 46–47
Hermans-Konopka, A. 46–47
hierarchical attitude 88, 100–101
Holocaust 140, 172
Hom, H. 90
homosexuality 57, 90–91
Hong Kong 14–15
Hong, Y.J. 117
Horowitz, Alexandra 123

human identity xx, 132, 133, 139–146, 149, 151, 178
Hyde, B. 108, 109

I-positions xvi–xvii, xxi, 3–10, 25, 62–63; boundaries of 14–16; changing perspective 27–28, 30–31; Composition Method 61n1; consumer-citizens 43–44, 149; dialogue with self 155–156; ecological responsibility 153; empathy 119–120, 121–122; four levels of inclusion 131, 133, 137, 139; inner contradiction 82; meta-positions 32–40, 48, 49, 62–63, 64, 72, 78, 119–120; multiple 5–6, 44, 143, 149, 150, 163; narcissism 168–169; open and closed minds 174–175; participation xx; self-agreements 71, 75; self-consultation 77; "talking stick" ritual 110; uncertainty 42, 46–47, 48–49; utopian thinking 172, 173
identity 8, 108–109, 178; consistent 12; ecological xiv, 132, 147–154; four levels of xx–xxi, 131–138; group xx, 99, 125, 131, 132, 133–138, 140, 142–143; human xx, 132, 133, 139–146, 149, 151, 178; individual xx, 132, 133, 149, 150, 151
immigrants 27, 57, 142, 143, 163
impersonal relations 169, 173, 175, 179
impulses 20, 117–118, 161
in-groups 47, 49, 98–102
inclusion, levels of xx, 132–133, 137, 139, 143–144, 149–152
individual level of inclusion xx, 132, 133, 149, 150, 151
individual (personal) responsibility xiv, xx, xxiv, 151
inner contradiction 34–36, 39, 50, 80–81, 82–83
inner democracy xvi, xxi, xxv, 62, 177; absence of inner opponent 89; contradiction 82–83; emotions 56; empathy 121–122; as learning process xviii, 167; listening to others 19; meta-positions 63; moral issues 92, 93; multiple *I*-positions 44, 150, 163; obstructions to 166–176, 179–180; opposition xvii–xviii, 29; promoting 155–165; school shooting perpetrators 135–136; self-agreements 70; suspension of judgment 21; tolerance of uncertainty 47, 65
inner dialogue xviii, xx, 50–51; contradiction 82; multiple *I*-positions 44;

192 Index

self-agreements 71, 75; self-criticism 73; self-exploration xvi; three-step model 48
inner opponent, absence of 89, 91, 92
insecurity 160, 168
internet 35
intolerance 57–58, 59, 65, 90, 92, 95
Islam 171, 173
Itzchakov, G. 80–82

Jacobs, M. 56
James, William 12
Jews 47, 57, 140
Johns, N. 45
Jones, S.B. 158
judgment: postponement of 125, 156, 170; suspension of 19–24, 48, 49, 63, 64, 157, 164; without knowledge 86–88
Jung, Carl 56
justice 150–151

Kahan, Dan 87, 100
Kassem, C.L. xxii
Kenen, Regina 71
Kilburn, D. 45
King, Martin Luther 141–142, 145
Kluger, A.N. 80–82
Knapp, M.L. 168–170
knowledge, judgment without 86–88, 91
Kolb, D.A. xxiii
Kross, E. 38
Kuitenbrouwer, Jan 112

learning: inner democracy 167; from others xviii, 125, 126; from yourself 69–78, 126
LeDoux, J. 55
Leuschner, V. 135–136
Lewis, Mark 73
listening 19–20, 21, 22, 63, 79–85, 126, 175; close relationships 167–168; dialogue 107–108, 126; empathy 125
Littler, J. 148–149
loners 136
Lovell, George 72

MacMath, S. xxi
Mandela, Nelson 7–8, 10n1, 141–142, 145
masculinity 135
master-terms 99, 127
McGregor, Sue 35
Meltzoff, A.N. 124n1
memory 98
Mersch, Ruben 91

meta-positions 32–40, 48, 49, 62–63, 64, 72, 78, 119–120
mindsets xxii
minimal group paradigm 133–135, 137, 178
minority groups 142–143, 150
moral equality xxi–xxii
moral opinions 86, 89–93, 95, 97, 125, 127
Moses, L.J. 116
multiculturalism xxii
multilevel citizenship xx–xxi
Murphy, Katy 167–168
music 120, 122, 146, 148–149

Naccache, L. 56
nanotechnology 86–87, 100–101
narcissism 168–170, 173, 179
Native American "talking stick" ritual 109–110, 113
Native Canadians 140
Nazism 171, 172, 173
Nederveen, Paul 148
negative emotions 37, 54–55, 59, 65, 88
neoliberalism 171, 172, 173
non-verbal communication 21, 23, 111

objective ambivalence 81–82, 83
obligations xviii–xix
open-mindedness, valley of 13, 16
open minds xxii, 14–15, 167, 173, 174–175
open positions 14, 16, 17, 29, 63
openness 109, 110–111
opinions xxi–xxii, 11–18; active listening 82; biased 94; changing perspective 25–31; depolarization 95–97, 101–102; dialogical capability 161–162; exclusive truth claims 166–167, 173; holding firmly to 29; lack of knowledge 87–88; moral 86, 89–93, 95, 97, 125, 127; suspension of judgment 19, 20, 22, 23; uncertainty 50; see also alternative points of view
opposition xvii–xviii, xxii, 29, 62, 94–104, 125, 177; see also contradiction; disagreement
Oreskes, N. 132
the other 6–8, 90–91, 97–98, 177; dialogue with 111–112; empathy 26; as multi-voiced 162–163
out-groups 47, 49, 98–100, 102

paradox of Solomon 38, 64
paraphrasing 96–97, 102–103, 176

participation xvii, xviii–xxi, xxii, 35, 155
Pasteur, Louis 71
Peffley, M. 56–57
Pelling, Mark 150–151
personal citizenship xvi
personal contact 97, 99, 102, 104
personal identity 108, 132; *see also* individual level of inclusion
personal (individual) responsibility xiv, xx, xxiv, 151
personal space 158, 169
perspective: changing 25–31, 48, 49, 108; perspective taking 116–117, 118, 123
The Pianist (movie) 140–141, 146
Plato 29, 53
pluralistic environment 101
polarization 82–83, 89, 94, 95, 99, 101–102
political tolerance 56–58
positioning 3–10; changing perspective 26, 27–28, 30–31; democracy as process of 172; emotion and reason 58; meta-positions 32–40, 48, 49, 62–63, 64, 72, 78, 119–120; moral positions 89–91; uncertainty 43; *see also* I-positions
prefrontal cortex 55
prejudice 47, 80, 99, 121, 141, 145
Prydz, Erik 149
purchasing behavior 44–46

questions, asking 21, 22, 23, 111, 175

race xvii, 143–144, 171
Rachman, Gideon 14–15
reason xvi, xviii, 52–61, 63
reflection xxii, xxiii, 33
rejection 135
religion 108, 171–172, 173
Republicans 88
respect 21, 22
responsibilities xiv, xix, xx, 44, 151–152, 178
Rezabakhsh, Behrang 35
rights xv, xviii, 56–57, 58
rigid boundaries 15–16, 155, 159, 164–165, 175; dialogical capability 162; exclusive truth claims 167, 173; in-groups and out-groups 47, 102; insecurity 160; social stereotypes 163
Rogers, Carl 80
Rohrschneider, R. 56–57
role-playing 120, 122

Rosenberg, E. 90
Roth-Hanania, R. 115–116

Scheithauer, H. 135–136
school shootings 135–136
self-agreements 69–70, 71, 74, 75–76
self-appraisals 136
self-consultation 70, 71–73, 74, 75, 76–77, 126
self-criticism 70, 73–74, 75, 77, 126
self-distance 37–39, 72
self-esteem 6, 12–13, 16, 108–109; counter-arguments 80; group identity 99, 134, 136; narcissism 168, 169; self-criticism 70, 74, 77; temporary reduction of 156
self-inflation 168–169, 173, 175, 179
self-reflection 55, 56
Shah, Sonia 149–150
social identity 132, 133–135, 137–138, 140, 178
social media 5–6, 13, 42, 105, 168
social rejection 135
social responsibility xiv, xx, xxiv, 151
soft boundaries 14, 16, 155, 158, 160, 162, 164–165, 175
Solomon, paradox of 38, 64
Sommer, F. 135–136
sponge-like boundaries 159, 160–161, 164–165, 175, 179
St. Paul (DJ) 148
stereotypes 47, 94, 99, 134, 162–163, 164, 175, 179
subjective ambivalence 81–82
summarizing 102–103, 125, 176
suspension of judgment 19–24, 48, 49, 63, 64, 157, 164
symbiotic relationships 14

Tajfel, H. 133–134
"talking stick" ritual 109–110, 113
task-oriented self-criticism 74, 75, 77
technology 42
theory of mind 116–117, 118, 122, 128
Thomassen, J. 58
three-step model 27–28, 29, 30, 48, 64, 108
tolerance xxii, 11–18; active listening 82, 83; political 56–58; of uncertainty 47–48, 112
transgender people 47
Tuller, H.M. 96, 103
Turner, J.C. 133–134
Twenge, J.M. 168, 173

uncertainty 12, 41–51, 63, 65, 112, 149
unconscious emotions 56
universal claims 89–90, 92, 125
utopian thinking 171–172, 173, 180

valley of open-mindedness 13, 16
values 17, 86–93, 109
Van Ham, C. 58
van Meijl, Toon 143, 163

Vangelisti, A.L. 168–170
Voltaire 29

we-positions xvi–xvii, xxi
Whelton, W.J. 73
Williams, S. 44–45
Wohl, M.J.A. 140
women 47, 89–90

Yousafzai, Malala 7–8, 10n2